COMMIE GIRL

IN THE OC

★ rebecca schoenkopf ★

V

VERSO

London • New York

First published by Verso 2008
Copyright © Rebecca Schoenkopf 2008
All rights reserved

The moral right of the author has been asserted

1 3 5 7 9 10 8 6 4 2

Verso
UK: 6 Meard Street, London W1F 0EG
USA: 180 Varick Street, New York, NY 10014-4606
www.versobooks.com

Verso is the imprint of New Left Books

ISBN-13: 978-1-84467-258-5

British Library Cataloguing in Publication Data
A catalogue record for this book is available from the British Library

Library of Congress Cataloging-in-Publication Data
A catalog record for this book is available from the Library of Congress

Typeset in Bell MT by Hewer Text UK Ltd, Edinburgh
Printed and bound in the USA by Quebecor World

contents

KEY

1. DISNEYLAND: *Need we say any more?*

2. YORBA LINDA: *Birthplace of Richard M. Nix 37th President of the United States. Now dead but yet still alive in so many ways.*

3. DOWNTOWN IRVINE: *Finally, money buys an escape from that pesky provincial past.*

4. SUBURBAN IRVINE: *Same, same, same. Beige, beige, beige. Thos monochrome vistas! That feeling of being watched!*

5. NEWPORT HARBOR: *(Shown larger than actual size. Reflects residents' opinions of selves.)*

13. HIGHLY COMBUSTIBLE REAL ESTATE: *Mega-acres of mega-expensive, mega-flammable homes.*

14. CITY OF FULLERTON: *Former Home of Fender Guitars, now Drinker's Mecca.*

15. LOS ALAMITOS: *Neigh! Check out nearby Bolsa Chica Wetlands!*

16. CITY OF STANTON: *Site of OC Sheriff Mike Carona's Catapult to Fame.*

17. TUSTIN BLIMP HANGARS: *Largest wooden structures anywhere. Ultimately doomed as all unique things here are to make way for the merely average.*

18. CITY OF SAN JUAN CAPISTRANO: *Home to historic 18th Century Mission, the swallows attendant thereto, and numerous cowboy bars.*

19. CITY OF SEAL BEACH: *Yes, it is in OC!*

20. IRVINE SPECTRUM GLOWING PHALLUS OF COMMERCE: *OK, it's an obelisk. Anything you say.*

21. SOUTH COAST PLAZA: *Because we couldn't afford the rights to depict Fashion Island.*

6. CITY OF SANTA ANA: Here be Mexicans. Thanks for the neat community names. Next, please.

7. ANGEL STADIUM OF ANAHEIM & HONDA CENTER: ...or whatever the hell they're calling themselves now. Active reminders that nothing's permanent.

8. JOHN WAYNE INTERNATIONAL AIRPORT: One million flights in and out of OC daily.

9. CITY OF HUNTINGTON BEACH: "Surf City, U.S.A." Huge, fuming conventional power plant. Restaurants. Nightlife. Babes.

10. POLLUTED, MUCKY WATER: Isn't there a Tom Lehrer line in here somewhere?

11. CITY OF LAGUNA BEACH: 200,000 Automobiles Never Tasted So Exclusive.

12. REAL HOUSEWIVES OF ORANGE COUNTY: Agonizing for the perfect footwear, or: Credit knows no limit if you're terrified your Republican husband might dump you for someone younger.

22. DANA POINT HARBOR: Another historic locale. Check out the Ocean Institute and Tall Ships!

23. CITY OF SAN CLEMENTE: Prime surfing spot and Nixon's California residence.

24. SAN ONOFRE NUCLEAR POWER FACILITY: A **totally** safe, clean, practically renewable symbolic balance to the Irvine Spectrum Obelisk.

preface

My Little Boy's First Gang!

Last week, for the tenth anniversary of the day he came to live with me, my small buttercup of a son got a punching bag and boxing gloves. I'm writing this two days before Christmas, and he still doesn't know that he'll be getting an air hockey table, minus the "air" part because it was the cheap one. He and his two friends from across the street have done amazing things to the garage already, where I informed him he could start a gang. They found carpets and posters, strung up purple Christmas lights and put a jar of snacks on the serape-covered, dilapidated round table, and now he's suggested a mini-fridge, though when I explained about energy consumption, he said a cooler would do. They're all yelling out there now, probably jumping in the girl who just moved next door. Please note I said "jumping in," not "jumping on." "Jumping in" is just a gang term for a bit of violent, bloody hazing. It's no big deal, just like Deke Week or Abu Ghraib.

His friends across the street are home-schooled, with all that implies, and are really great, well-mannered boys. Once I gave them $5 to feed my dog when I was away for the weekend, and they also brushed her, played with her and picked up her poo. I'm a good neighbor; I respect the boys' parents and haven't once sat those kids down to talk evolution.

If anyone deserves a gang, it's these three. They just now decided they're washing my car.

*

My first Christmas with my son, he was eighteen months old. If I took him into work with me at the just-founded *OC Weekly* in Orange County, California, I could perch him on a stool and never worry about him toppling; he never moved an inch. My stepmom, his mother, had died of AIDS, and before she did, she was medicated most of the time, so movement on his part wasn't encouraged. It simply wouldn't have been safe, so he sat on the bed with the television, humming to keep himself company. After my stepmom died, my dad, in his grief, wasn't caring much for the baby, so my boyfriend and I took him for the weekend and never gave him back. Eight days later, it was Christmas. The three of us lived in a one-room studio, with a two-foot tree hung with my earrings and the toys Jimmy had brought with him gathered beneath. I tried the same trick for years—putting things he already owned along with his presents, so it looked greater and more bountiful, until about four years ago when he wised up. He was righteously pissed about it, too. This year, there's bounty. A ten-foot tree in a two-story house. Hockey and iPods and the Gorillaz and Johnny Cash, the Man in Black, intoning that he's "Hurt." There's $1 Store crap that won't last a week, straight from a sweatshop to us, but that looks nice and plentiful in its pile. I don't feel guilty about showering my boy with items; it's not like when we lived in the ghetto and I had to remind myself, when faced with the neighbor kids' jealousy, wonder and awe, that having our own rooms—Jimmy in his, I in mine—was no luxury. In *Vanity Fair*, Wm Thackeray goes to town on London's own conspicuous Newport set, but there's nothing wrong, he says, with a good roast, a warm fire and a nice claret.

I haven't liked Orange County much lately. It took me ten years to realize I was wrong: OC *is* just as conservative as the stereotype, which I'd denied up and down to anyone listening. Hell, I was surrounded by right-thinking folks at the *Weekly* and consorted only with museum types, punks and drunkards. John Birch is dead. Long live *la raza!*

It took Señor Schwarzenegger's propositions, overwhelmingly denied through the rest of the state and overwhelmingly approved here, to make me see just how willingly I'd blinded myself. It's not the conservatism that bothers me: it's the nastiness. The nattering classes I'd thought were fringey were in fact the opinion-makers. The Scrooges on the local blogs went to war lest the OC Board of Supes approve lone Democrat Lou Correa's motion to insure twenty thousand of the county's poorest kids with an outlay of just $2.1 million. It would, they fumed, create an *entitlement*. Now, how many millions do you think the supes spend on mailings?

Listen, I don't like to hang out with poor people any more than the rest of y'all. They're often boorish and usually distressingly uneducated, which leads to really boring conversation. And when Stevie Wonder sang, "Her clothes are old, but never are they dirty," well, how would Mr Wonder know? But they will always be among us. I know 'cause Jesus said so.

Why did the media stop demanding a death toll in Katrina? Why did the government stop searching the attics? Why was it so easy for us, after a week of horror, to put it aside for the next piddling story just because the next hurricane came and uneventfully went? Why the fuck doesn't anyone care?

I never thought I'd be happier to see a year end than when I was almost rid of 2001. But then 2005 didn't look much better. I didn't even care that people were finally starting to talk about "impeachable offenses." Really, name one that *wasn't*.

When I go to San Francisco to see my brother's new baby, I hate it just as much there, but for totally different reasons. And then I come back, drinking and fighting, with my girl gang all around me. Give us a call: we'll jump you in if you want.

SeCTiON ONe:

I Hate People

careless people

**The Real Housewives of Orange County aren't different from you and me—
I have met them, and they are us**

Falling Safes

It was one of those safes falling on you from a third-story window, a cartoon moment of consciousness-flattening, tweeting bluebirds and epiphany. And it happened as I watched the seven magnificent episodes of the newest voyeuristic reality show, *The Real Housewives of Orange County*.

It happened as I sat glued to the merry adventures of Kim, Jo, Lauri, Vicki and Jeana in one seven-episode marathon.

"Perception is reality," Bree said on *Desperate Housewives—The Real Housewives ur* text—just this past Sunday, clearly providing her answer to the Kantian question, "What are the powers and capacities constitutive of the human subject for apprehending the Real?"

Perception. Image. Get used to it: you may think the world's view of Orange County depends only on that small segment pictured in the party pages of *Riviera*, but they are the ones who are real; the rest of us—we who live in Anaheim and Santa Ana instead of Newport and Laguna Beach, who are of color, or at least brunette, instead of entitled blond society misses with pillowy lips at play in the fields of South Coast Plaza, who are poor or middle-class and have as little to do with the charity dos and parties in jewelry stores as the rich have to do with day laboring at Home Depot or shopping at Target—

we are Schrödinger's cat, in a tertiary position between existing and not. Without the world's eyeballs, the rest of us simply aren't.

So now, three years into the nation's love affair with greed and tanned young idiots—*The OC, Orange County* (the movie), *Laguna Beach: The Real Orange County,* even the parodic *Arrested Development*—who are our newest spokesmodels?

The *Real Housewives* introduce us.

There's Kimberly, the outgoing transplant who—even while making sure we knew she was above all that silliness—dived right into the bleach and implants of her new home.

There's Jo, the young party girl fiancée of Hummer-driving Slade—think *DH*'s Gabrielle sans the calculation and if she ever smiled or was kind.

There's Lauri, the divorcée who no longer has the lifestyle of her friends.

There's Vicki, for whom Lauri works selling insurance, and who is both self-made and a terrible control freak.

There is Jeana, a plump former Playmate who sells real estate and gives homespun advice in a flat, affectless voice.

There are various husbands. There are misbegotten spawn. And there is the hive, its own organism, where they all (except Lauri) live: the rarefied hills of Coto de Caza.

Coto de Caza is the ne plus ultra of Orange County—an actual gated town. But unlike the swarming developments spreading across the rest of South County, the manses of Coto were actually developed gracefully, nestled into folds in the hills so nothing mars the ridgelines or the sky. Most of the mansions actually have breathing room—an acre here, an acre there—instead of million-dollar homes built within inches of their lot lines. These are proper mansions, nothing Mc- or chintzy about them. And behind its gates, Coto even still has an orange grove. Coto's a pretty sweet place to live, if you like marble, and beige, and children driving brand-new Mercedes.

And if you, like I, like to watch rich people behaving badly—and is there any other explanation for the popularity of Donald Trump?—you'll like Coto just as much.

And you, like I, will realize that these people *are* the true Orange County, just as J. R. was the soul of Dallas, and Kurt Cobain really was Seattle.

Do Not Read This Part Of The Story

The following will be one long, giant spoiler of everything of interest that happens on this season of *The Real Housewives of Orange County*—and everything that happens is of interest. Every one of you should stop reading immediately.

Episode One: Jeana's children are monsters! Jeana's husband is a monster! Jeana (our plump real-estate agent) is no great shakes herself! Jeana's daughter Kara whines soulfully when her older brother Shane gets a new car and she has to drive his hand-me-down convertible Mercedes. Shane grunts angrily when Kara gets cold hard cash for making the volleyball team. Kara demands a new car. Kara gets a new car. Meanwhile, Shane gets drafted by the Oakland A's in, like, the 1,000th round, and dad Matt Keough, who used to play for the A's and still works in the organization, calls home to find out how the draft went. Father and son share a monosyllabic conversation. "I think he's proud of you," Jeana says, noncommittally, flatly and without affect, after the phone call. "He thought you were going to do a lot worse."

Kimberly (our outgoing transplant) makes fun of how everyone in OC has breast implants. But Kimberly likes her own breast implants. We call this "cognitive dissonance."

Slade wants 24-year-old party girl fiancée Jo to stay home and be a housewife. The camera lingers as she sits on the kitchen counter, staring at the phone, wondering what the fuck she's going to do with her day.

Vicki (self-made insurance lady) is a bitch, and Lauri (the broke-ass divorcée who suffers under her) is a victim.

Episode Two: Jeana's son Shane goes off to kill some bunnies for the neighbors, who are tired of replacing their impatiens. He has an arsenal at his disposal, but it's a lot of Elmer Fudd for nothing. No rabbits were harmed in the making of this series.

Kim goes to buy a new car. "*I* don't care about my car," she says, not at all shallow like her neighbors, "but in *this* area . . ." But oh, as the car salesman is showing her all the great places to stow your kids in the SUV, he lets fly with "grandchild," as in, "Here would be a great place to put your grandchild." Everything stops for the smallest of most perfect beats. Kim does not buy the car.

Slade, who is a freak, does tai chi in his underwear and what appears to be an ice mask to reduce puffiness before showing us his power outfits for his big meeting. He yammers on about needing to appear wealthy so the dude he's meeting will know he's capable of . . . what? Being wealthy? Then he climbs into a Hummer, and I laugh and laugh. But then he meets with the guy, and the guy is so unbelievably rude I thought it was a put-up job. I mean, no one acts that way. Not even Trump times ten acts that way. The guy is seriously, seriously damaged—and wait till you meet his wife, who puts cubic zirconia on the pink rims of her monster truck! The wife is really pretty awesome.

Lauri notes, about being rich, "I really miss those things. *I'm* the maid now." The observant viewer will note her Mizrahi bedding, which I saw on my shopping sojourn through Target just today. It's cute—giant orange blossoms, splashy and colorful—but again, if Lauri still had her status, she would only shop at Target for the maid's bedding. Which, of course, I guess she did.

Vicki's son Michael is an asshole.

Jeana's son Shane is an asshole. But let me elaborate: Shane and his little brother Colton, who is thirteen, are in Mexico with their family and go to some dirt-racing track. Colton stalls his dune buggy thingie a bunch of times—because he is thirteen—before he gets it right. He then beats Shane's time on the track. Shane's only possible recourse is to keep making fun of him for stalling. "It's my first time driving a stick, Shane!" Colton points out sensibly. "Come on, give me a little credit!" Shane grunts angrily and, like an asshole, says, "The first time *I* drove a stick, it was a *Ferrari*."

Lauri's daughter Ashley is an asshole, but that doesn't come till episode four, and I'm tired of recapping the episodes, and I will stop.

Except for this: Lauri's son Josh actually seems like a sweet kid, so he spends most of the season in juvie. It seemed like the teacher he scuffled with was the asshole, but it was off camera, so we'll never really know. In any case—go juvenile justice system!—they kept him doped up in juvenile hall to make sure he didn't have a mental illness *for more than a month* before they sentenced him to an additional month because he'd been caught with pot in the past. So when he calls home, all lonely and fucked-up and locked away while big sister Ashley is having a party, she hears his voice and instantly hangs up on him with the same guilty manner with which you hang up if a woman answers when you call her boyfriend. *That was my little brother calling from juvenile hall,* she tells her friend bemusedly. *Should I have talked to him, do you suppose?*

A Literary Interlude, Citing Fitzgerald

The very rich are different from you and me, Ernest Hemingway said—appropriating the thought, almost to the word, from F. Scott Fitzgerald. (Fitzgerald had said, "Let me tell you about the rich. They are different from you and me," which, you will notice, is almost just exactly the same!) But Fitzgerald had whole books of thought on the subject, while Hemingway mostly wrote about fish. Fitzgerald's most famous novel, *The Great Gatsby*, has probably even been read by the dimwitted offspring of *The Real Housewives of Orange County*. I wonder what they made of this:

> They were careless people, Tom and Daisy—they smashed up things and creatures and then retreated back into their money or their vast carelessness, or whatever it was that kept them together, and let other people clean up the mess they had made. . .

Barbarians At The Gates

I drove behind the gates of Coto de Caza last week to meet with the women—all except Jeana, who was out of town seeing her asshole son, who's playing ball at an Arizona community college. The country club where we coffee'd was hushed, even desolate on a rainy morning—the dark woods you would expect, the sweet selection of teas. Framed in the ceiling-high windows behind the women's heads, the ridgelines of Coto de Caza were perfectly populated—not too many houses, or too few. It still had the natural beauty you'd expect of John Wayne's old hunting grounds—his *actual* hunting grounds, not the bars of Balboa.

The women were nice, and ladylike, and funny and outgoing, and they looked far prettier in person than on the telly. Kim had looked manly on the TV; in person her features were softer and sexy. Lauri had looked plastic, the light and video catching awkwardly on what seemed to be less-than-organic features; at the table at the Coto country club, she was gorgeous. Vicki still looked like a rabbit, but I probably would have found her less rabbity if I had liked her as a person.

Vicki was a trial. She instructed the others not to answer questions about themselves she'd deemed too personal and tried to micromanage everything, from what photos we would be using to how much Kim should talk.

Outgoing Kim was saying something outgoing—perhaps it was after I'd complimented her for going out with her girlfriends and dancing and flirting with little people and people in wheelchairs (I thought that was nice!) and she'd responded outgoingly, "I am very much an equal opportunist!" So naturally Vicki sniped, "Oh, it's the Kim Show again." Kim thanked her genuinely for reining her in, said she was well aware that she often needed it, and apologized sweetly for monopolizing (she wasn't) the conversation. She begged to hear what Vicki had to say. "Nothing, really," Vicki answered peevishly. "I don't really have a piece to say."

Not only was she schoolmarming Kim, she was treating me as if I were her eighteen-year-old daughter—the same daughter she tried to browbeat into quitting her job rather than missing a family weekend at their second home (they have four) at the River. To her husband's credit, he firmly (for him) explained that quitting your job for a weekend's play is not a good life lesson for a teenager.

My sources also tell me that, after I left, Vicki demanded of the Bravo publicist, who was in attendance with the series producer as we all had coffee and fruit, that Bravo pay for a $150 flower arrangement Vicki had bought for her coffee table in anticipation of a visit from *Access Hollywood*. As a person who makes a good, decent middle-class living—an income that, if the Real Housewives were making it, would probably drive them to bankruptcy—I would like to say that I frequently buy myself flowers because it makes my house look nice. And I have never, not once, demanded someone else pay for them. But maybe that's how you get four houses.

On Subjectivity

And here is my reality: I try never to interview anyone, because when they are nice people and I like them, I feel compelled to soften my impressions, to treat them kindly, to present them under a warmish amber light—to mediate their reality for the world. At our group roundtable, I am open to the possibility that the perception is *not* reality, that someone got a villain edit in the series. After all, if a camera crew were shadowing me, it would show me yelling at my son, ignoring my son, snapping at my son, and watching television for many hours each night as I lie in bed and fart, and it would be both true and untrue.

It would not show me *boiling hot dogs* for dinner, as some of the Real House-wives are wont to do (perhaps it's a Midwestern thing?). But none of us is perfect. Most of the women are fun, nice and pretty, though they fall into the categories of either ditzy or ballbusters. They're warm. And their manners, almost to the person, are the best manners of all: they try to make people feel at home.

So what if their worlds are really, really small, I tell myself. Not everyone likes to dance in conga/protest lines outside white-power shows. Some people like to play tennis and buy their children new cars! And that's . . .

Fuck, that's really not okay.

Those kids are little Hitlers.

Is it the fault of their mothers? Yes. They play them off each other, they reward shrill whining by kowtowing to it, they work all the livelong day to give their children "the best" of everything—diamond shopping here is a bonding experience, like hunting might be for boys and their fathers among the Maori—while their rude, lazy children spit with contempt right in their faces.

They have raised their children not to become citizens, but consumers: they are entitled to anything they want.

But while we love to watch bad parenting—*Nanny 911, Anna Nicole*—softened reality swoops down again. My own sweet son (who is honestly terribly sweet) has not yet reached the age when boys become dicks. Perhaps he will spit at me. Perhaps he will grow up to be an Orange County boy—his life's goal so far *is* to own a mansion. He has expensive tastes, loves caviar and aches for golden bling. And while he knows better than to whine around me, I've heard tell he's done so before more receptive audiences. Someday he may even drive a Hummer, if only to give his poor mother a stroke. And maybe then, in the world's eyes, he will Exist.

Warriors, Come Out to Play

I was having, how do you say, a snit.

I wanted to go to the Russian Culture Expo on the *Queen Mary*. My boyfriend did not.

"Why don't *you* just go?" he asks.

"Because I don't want to be alone with a bunch of scary Russian men who're all, *Hello, I'm Russian*," I answer.

He would go if I wanted to. If I really, really wanted to, he would go. If I really wanted to.

"What would *you* like to do tonight?" I ask solicitously, keeping my patience.

"Anything," he says.

"Like what?" I ask.

"Anything you want," he says.

I don't remind him that he clearly doesn't want to do *anything* I want, since he clearly doesn't want to go to the Russian Culture Expo on the *Queen Mary*.

"I don't want to go anywhere," I spit. "I just want to stay home!" I put on my pajamas, grab my Harry Potter and seethe on the bed. It is nine o'clock on a Saturday night.

So what does he do? He sits down at the computer in the other room and doesn't pay one lick of attention to the fact that I am seething in my pajamas at nine o'clock on a Saturday night. *Tap-tap-click*, I hear. Great.

Ass.

"Okay," he says, finally showing his face. "There aren't any square dances this week, but the roller rink has an adult session tonight. Would you like to go roller-skating with me?"

"You looked up square dances?" I ask.

"Yeah, but there aren't any this week," he answers.

"You looked up square dances *for me?*"

I am a melty pile of puppy love.

By the time we get to the Holiday roller rink in Orange, I am furious. The night is warm and lovely, my boyfriend is kind and quiet, and I have thrown away the cigarettes he caught me with after a week of abstaining strong and tall. Now I am whiny and kvetchy. I'm not a good roller skater. I don't know how. I'm not coordinated and I'm gonna fall.

We get inside. I pout.

We put our skates on. I sulk.

We glide out onto the gorgeous wood floor—it looks like rich Hawaiian koa—scarred with decades of burns and pits and a few buckling deathtraps. I am mortified—I don't know how to unlock my knees, and I'm fucking fat!

Look how fucking fat I am!

And he grabs my hand and it's magic, and I shriek, and it's scary, and we go slow and retarded. Whenever our hands get sweaty I laugh and push him away and then move my arms in big, giant circles, trying to keep my balance by doing imaginary retarded aerobics as I skate. *Whoosh,* we go fast, like on Thunder Mountain—who knew it was only twenty-eight miles an hour? It only takes twenty minutes to unclench my knees. This is fun!

There are half a dozen eighteen-year-old hotties—white girls who manage to be both skinny and have big, J. Lo-style bubble butts. Since when can white girls grow asses like that? They are there for Melinda's birthday, we know, because the DJ keeps announcing it and there are fewer than thirty people here all together. Two of them look like twins, one in a white tank and her spitting image in black. The good twin, who's gorgeous, smiles when we make accidental eye contact. How sweet, she smiled at the old fat lady in her fat pants! The evil twin keeps dancing sexy while she skates. Often, she bends over, busting slightly heavy-metal rock star moves and throwing the devil horns. She reminds me of Steven Tyler. Oh, I hate her so, me and my graceless knock-knees.

Knock-knees, by the way, make you look even fucking fatter, you disgusting fucking blob.

And then it's wonderful again, and I am complaining about the girls making me feel old as if I'm Sandra Tsing Loh carrying on about her crow's feet, and my boyfriend is perfect and does not look at them except to make fun. And there are boys line-dancing on their skates, skating backward, fast, in a perfect row in perfect rhythm, and my boyfriend after many, many loops around the rink manages to hop backward and make some faces, and he acts like he isn't proud and that this is all gay, but you don't see him *not* skating backward!

He does dancey moves too, again with the I'm-kidding face, the same one I put on when I bend my fat ass over and throw the devil horns and say, "Wait, wait! Who am I?" and he says, "Steven Tyler?" and I say, confused, "Did you say 'Jimmy Carter'?" and he says, "Wait, do it again," and I do it again and he says, "George McGovern?" and we laugh because we are *hilarious*.

And now we're going faster. We start passing people sometimes, the people like us who aren't good at this. The hot teens pass us many times, and I'm sick with hate and envy at their easy sluttiness and my matronly hair. They look like the Hilton sisters. The ref-shirted DJ takes a break from the booth and dance-skates, suave and rhythmic. A slight, Kris Kristofferson-haired fortysomething in an open shirt dance-skates, suave and rhythmic. A tight brunette with "Orange County" across her huge bosoms dance-skates, suave and rhythmic. Some folks with a whiff of the trailer about them cruise through, graceful and fluid like they probably are nowhere else. Life is good here, at the Holiday. The good twin hangs out with someone who looks like someone's mom. The evil twin bends over. Off in a corner of the floor, the tattooed, built young gangsta in the wife-beater and baggy pants (one of the line dancers, or "flea hoppers"), sits, pensive, chin on fist, like The Thinker. J. Lo comes over the speakers. The young man nods, still contemplating, before his head, unbidden, does the *Night at the Roxbury* bop.

Every time I look at the evil twin I lose my burgeoning rhythm and gauchely almost fall. I envy everyone's ease. "Yeah, but they're all *regulars*!" my boyfriend says. "They're all *skating dorks*." So what? What exactly is wrong with being a skating dork? I want to come back again and again and get good at this, like the trailer folk. "(You Spin Me) Right Round" comes on, and there's a nasty spill between one of the speed skaters and a friend of the hotties. Their friends all crowd around, for minutes, and the DJ shuts the music down. We cackle and whisper; they were all *hopped up* on the *eighties music!* We imitate angry parents suing Metallica. The next time an eighties song comes on, we look at each other fearfully. Nobody seems to crash into anyone else during the hip hop.

The mural in the snack bar advises, "Let's Party!" Some little kids watch, patient, even though they're not allowed on the floor. But then Duran Duran start up with "Rio" and I glide around feeling like a sexy junior high school girl who's all good at skating and stuff until I get a look at the evil twin's ass, which is sticking up in the air because she's bent over again, and I lose my mojo and almost fall. They make us skate counterclockwise then. It's unnatural!

We are gleefully in love and happy. At about 11:15, our feets hurting, we call it a night and happily bop out to the parking lot. By the time we get home ten minutes later, I am furious and won't get out of the car.

I'm smoking right now, just to get my work done, but then I'm throwing them away.

You know. Like a bad habit.

warriors for christ

It might have been the best night of my life, Friday, if one could say that about a night where no one was naked. Not only were Suzette and I the comeliest lasses at Costa Mesa's Harp Inn, a perfect daydream of a place with handsome young men out trawling for trouble and friendly, social girls clustered in the ladies', not only were there interludes of bloody filet mignon at La Cave, and not only did we have each other (I got you, babe!) but we got, as we long to do, to fight. (The next night I tried to fight snotty artrepreneur Ed Giardina at the Artists' Village First Saturday opening, but it wasn't really the same.)

You maybe can't tell it from looking at us—we so classy!—but Suzette and I are always just one ill-considered word from a bloody pile-on, eagle-eyed in our lookout for wrongs that must be righted with our stiletto tongues. We are, like that craaaazy screaming lady on *Trading Spouses*, Warriors. Warriors for Christ, maybe, or perhaps good manners, or just truth, justice and the American way.

But on to our tale. After closing down the Harp with a hundred of our new best friends, after dancing to the choice cover selections of the Creepers imbued, Bloodhound Gang-style, with lots of nasty lyrical reworkings (I guess the Violent Femmes' "Blister in the Sun" does lend itself to masturbatory imagery, now that I think on it), after drinking our fair share and making eyes at and giving our digits to predatory men, we were invited to an after-party full of handsome young Irishmen, a few Costa Mesa local yokels, and some various girlfriends and neighbors.

Do we want to go to an after-party? You betcha!

Between the front house and the back house on a Costa Mesa lot near the Harp was a pimped outdoor living room, with velvet couches, tenting, a TV for satellite, radios and a bar. It was very dated-OC-hipster-clothing-company Black Flys, and pretty damn perfect for post-2 a.m. We sat, ladylike, on the couches in a corner, drinking a beer and chatting. Were we hoochie-mamma-ed out? We might have been mistaken for the Amish. Were we pole dancing? Not in the least. Were we within 20 feet of "Johnny," who lived there with his girlfriend, "Lucia," and another friend, "Brian"? In fact, we weren't; "Johnny" was across the room, sipping his beer without a care in the world. Which is why when "Lucia" came home and started screaming that we were fucking bitches she didn't know and we could get the fuck out of her fucking house, Suzette and I were delighted. It's always good to have the unassailable moral high ground in any situation. You know: like the Bush administration when it comes to torture.

"I know *you!* And I know *you!*" shouted "Lucia"—aw, fuck it; her name's actually Lucia—to a couple of girls who were there with their boyfriends. "*But,*" and here Scarface put her fingers in our faces. "I don't know this fucking bitch! And I don't know this fucking bitch!"

"I'm Suzette," said Suzette after an ironic moment or two, and graciously stuck out her hand.

"I don't care who the fuck you are. I don't like fucking bitches I don't know in my fucking house!" Lucia predictably screamed.

"Um, she's with me, Lucia," Brian whispered, seeing as how it was his house too. Until then I wasn't aware there are men who will let their roommates' girlfriends determine their guest list, but clearly Brian had already learned the first rule of abuse: the hand goes up, the mouth goes shut. She looked at me. "And you!" she shrilled at me, gesturing to an Irish kid sitting next to me on the couch. "Are *you* with him?!?"

"Yeah, sure," I replied, out-ironicizing Suzette by five. I win!

Well, then, everything was peaches and cream! Lucia sat herself down on Suzette's lap and started kissing her on the cheek. "I'm sorry I was rude," she said charmingly, and I could almost hear, "You know I love you, baby, but why do you have to make me so mad?" But it was better. She continued. "I can't help it. I'm just a bitch!"

Ah. The old "I'm just a bitch." Possibly the finest excuse in history for one's unavoidable, can't-help-it behavior besides "we need every weapon in our arsenal in the war against terror."

If there's one thing George Bush and I have in common, it's our dislike of those who don't take personal responsibility for their actions. And blaming her actions on "just who she is," as if "who she is" somehow wasn't attributable to her at all, well, it was almost as bad as when, in the next breath, she said, "I can't help it! I'm Mexican!"

Oh, no, she didn't.

Oh, yes, she did.

I gave Lucia my well-considered thoughts on the subject, most of them having to do with my own experiences of the brand of hospitality proffered by the Latinas I have known (usually including pan dulce), the inaccuracies in her cultural stereotyping (jealousy I could see—I'd just seen *Tosca* with my dad the night before—but unladylike rudeness? Never), the wisdom of abusing everyone in sight, the unfeasibility of psychosis as a solution to keeping your relationship spicy, and the fact that as far as I had been able to divine, nobody wanted her boyfriend but her. I didn't have a chance to add that there are many who interpret the story of Sodom and Gomorrah as God striking down the cities not for their sexual and homosexual license but because the citizens thereof treated strangers with a lack of hospitality. I figured that might be getting a little abstruse.

"If you don't like it, you can get the fuck out of my fucking house!" she rejoined, and we did, although not before we ceded a small bit of our moral high ground when Suzette's switch flipped a 180 and she stood, the better to look down from her six-foot-one and threaten to kick Lucia's ass, which, frankly, since we were in fact in her fucking house, I didn't completely approve of, but at least Suzette had done *something*, unlike all the cowering men who kept whispering to us, "You do not want to argue with her. You won't win."

What do you tell a man with two black eyes?

Nothing. You told him twice already.

nascar weekend

The publicist from the National Association for Stock Car Auto Racing was on my phone. "We thought you might like to do a story on how NASCAR is now becoming more diverse," she was chirping as I was vomiting into the nearest receptacle.

"Um, we don't cover Fontana," I excused, which is true as long as it's not local cowboy/carpenter/legend Chris Gaffney *singing* about Fontana ("I saw your brother yesterday, he's a loser/Living in Fontana with a kitchen for his farm"), in which case we cover it every time, but what I didn't want to say flat out was that we don't do stories publicists hand us. Just ask Nikki Finke and her friends at *Vanity Fair*!

"Well, what *do* you write about?" the nice flack wanted to know, and it's always a difficult question to answer.

"Well, you know, like, what I did that week? And places I went? And some stuff about the President?" It never sounds very impressive when I put it that way.

Oh, but this one, she was sly. She had an answer for everything. "Well, would you like to come be in someone's pit crew for the day? Would that work?"

Honey, why didn't you say so in the first place?

And that's the not-terribly-scintillating tale of how I became a part of Scott Riggs' pit crew at NASCAR's Nextel Cup on Saturday. My job? To not get anyone killed. Duck and cover, everybody!

The night before, I'd done shots at the velvet-walled oldster lounge the Fling, and the night before that, I'd crashed a toga party for Kappa Tau, so my weekend was catching up to me when I hit the area code that was the 909. After an hour-and-38-minute attempt to drive the final two-tenths of a mile to the freeway offramp, I was really, really late. Then I got lost four times trying to find the correct gate and the tunnel to the infield. The constant calls to my media handler and the embarrassing inability to get there from here (one of Commie Mom's favorite lacerating sayings? "Aw, you just can't get there from here." It's deadly!) were not auguring well for my stint on Pit Road. Hell, by the time I got there (from here), I was so sweaty and my jeans were so stuck to me I couldn't even swing my legs over the two-foot-high wall separating Pit Road from the stalls *when I was sitting on it.* It took a good two minutes of huffing and puffing and pitying looks. This, like Darrell Issa's gubernatorial candidacy, was all going to end in tears.

Luckily, I had a new flack in Tara, a North Carolina gal who's been traveling with NASCAR for three years, knows everybody, is plainspoken and warm, explained all the NASCAR mysteries down to the last flipdiddle (that's the scientific term for them), and let me follow her around for seven hours like a retarded puppy.

Wait, Tara! Wait for me!

Also, I got a headset. Yay!

Very little actually happens during a 250-lap, 500-mile race, and once the merciless sun goes down and that sweet Fontana breeze starts to blow (I smell Chino!), it's actually very Zen. Even with the cast of *Herbie Goes Bananas Yet Again and One More Time* in the pit stall next to ours, things weren't, you know, *exciting*.

Now, with Herbie going nuts and all, I was waiting to see Matt Dillon because when I used to live in New York City, I used to see him all the freaking time, and I would get this mortifying instant Tourette's. "*Fuck you,* Matt Dillon!" I would spit as we walked toward each other on the street. "Think you're so fucking cool, Matt Dillon! Fuck you! SUCK COCK!" It was really weird.

So this time, I wanted to tell Matt Dillon, tenderly, to fuck off for old time's sake or maybe, like my new and spitty hero Zell Miller, challenge him to a duel, but sadly it was not to be. Instead I just hung out with my Valvoline posse, and time and again as Herbie's "pit crew" hopped (hopped!) up and down and clasped their hands together like girls who'd just gotten a bunny and gently patted one another's backs in celebration, we would watch with joyously jaded derision. "Wow, they've won, like, four times now," one girl said. "They must be really good."

Ho ho ho! What a bitch!

I wish I'd said it.

Fucking Matt Dillon thinks he's so cool.

Ah, the good old days. On this day, appropriately, I was even wearing my I Love New York baby-T, which didn't get Matt Dillon's attention because he's way too fucking cool for that but led lots of tall and tanned and swaggery men to tell me, "Ah *loh-ove* New York," as though, well, I don't know how to describe it for an audience that will so often come on to a woman by asking her classily to sit on its collective face. Let's just say it's all about subtext and mystery and restraint, and there was more blatant sexing in those words than in *Tropic of Cancer* or Lynne Cheney's *Sisters*. "Ah *loh-ove* New York"? Baby, I love me some freakin' NASCAR!

So we smoked a lot of cigarettes and waited for cars to wreck and every half hour or so put some new tires on the car real, *real* fast and tried to keep hydrated and sat on a wall. I can't imagine how lame it must be in the stands, but backstage? Honey, you're special. You get a headset.

That was pretty much it, except we came in seventh, which is supergood, and Scott Riggs was pretty darling as was every last member of his crew, and they all want me to come to North Carolina to visit—like you could freaking stop me!—and baby, they *loh-ove* New York.

The most Horrible man in the world

He was the only guy at Coconuts who didn't have a whiff of vomit on his breath while the 5150s—three middle-aged gutty dudes—did guitar-god headbanging to their "classic rock," such as "Pink Cadillac" and "Mustang Sally." During "Margaritaville," a tiny brunette mom-type got onstage and, with the world's most blissful smile, did that boob-shakey thang, while two tweaker ladies with methamphetamine-induced circles round their eyes that made Al Pacino look like a Maybelline spokesmodel danced all over the floor, sticking their bottoms up in the air like they just didn't care.

San Clemente is a pit.

My sister and I had already spent some quality time at Big Helyn's, the county's southernmost bar. There Elsa, the owner/bartendress, was a vision of dominatrixy retro; we liked her, and we liked the crowd (they welcome a lot of homeless people into their fold), but for a Marine bar, it didn't have very cute boys. That's the thing about San Clemente: you always think the people will be more attractive in this lazy beach town, and you're always surprised when they're not. I swear, it's like hanging out in Fontana.

We moved on to the Outrigger, where a crazy tweaker rested his eyeballs on the smoking patio's TV screen, flipping the channels as fast as he could count and talking to either the TV, himself or God.

So by the time we hit Coconuts and saw a guy there whose eye whites weren't a pretty shade of pink, our standards had fallen away like religious Republicans voting for Arnold Schwarzenegger. He wasn't noticeably drunk, he wasn't twitching, and he was from Oregon. People from Oregon are nice! So even after nodding and smiling our way through a five-minute conversation about drywall suppliers, we still invited him to join us at our favorite South County redneck/felon/two-step bar, the Swallow's.

It seemed in addition to his drywall business, Ladd had busted bulls on a ranch in Oregon, been head loader for the Peter Britt Festival, had four black belts and was a hairdresser/DJ. Which was all good and fine, but when my sister mentioned her belts in Eagle Claw, he left her hanging on the high-five while he explained that he himself had *four* belts in it; he'd learned from his uncle, a grand master who had studied under Bruce Lee. And when he said he'd "hung out" with Bob Dylan after loading his gear (because if there's one thing Bob Dylan is, it's approachable with roadies), and I mentioned that our dad used to be Bob Dylan's roommate, he at first ignored it and then told me he wasn't impressed by people who tried to impress him. "After Willie Nelson's stopped his bus and everyone's gone, 'Ladd, get on the bus!' you're not impressed when people try to impress you," he said to me, really very impressively.

I didn't make the mistake of mentioning any of my very famous friends. You know I don't like to show off!

A solid hour later, we had learned that Ladd used to live in Bullhead City and would take the bus (it only cost $5) over to the Riverboat Casino, where he would come with $100 and leave with $180, except for the time he came with $10 and in six hours made $90, and once he made $340. After he'd blathered on for ten minutes with two nice drunks at the Swallow's about their shared English heritage, I mentioned mine: half Russian-Polish Jew and half English/Irish/Scottish/German. A few minutes later, when Sarah and I asked pointedly if perhaps he would like to ask us something about *us* and then showed him how by asking conversational questions about *him*, his only question was "Nice heritage." Huh? "You know, the comment you made before that was totally irrelevant to the conversation we were having?" Oh, yes. That heritage. My apologies, Ladd!

Sarah and I had already had some fun dancing with ourselves in the Swallow's cattle call—it was packed with fun in there, and it allowed us to avoid our now-unwanted guest—but we kept going back for more and more Ladd. It was just like when you're 'shrooming, and there's a vortex in the kitchen, and the vortex is scary, but you keep going back for more scary kitchen vortex. You know?

What would Ladd say next?

We kept trying. Would Ladd respond to *anything* we said, or would he just keep looking perturbed at the interruptions? Ladd was a very serious man! We decided to save Ladd from having to try to show interest in what we had to say; it was just too hard for him. So we offered without prompting the story of our lives: how we'd grown up in Iowa with our dad, who was a professor of English history, and how idyllic our childhood was with dad studying in the den and coming out to say fatherly things like, "Now, children! Please try to shush!" At that point, Ladd asked his first question of the evening. "You're sisters?" It had only taken him two hours.

We continued with our childhood happiness: how our two moms had been able to complement each other so well, with Sarah's mom bringing in hard cash as a corporate attorney while my mom baked and hung out with all the wives' children. "There were a couple of others, too—younger women—but they were more like our sisters," I told Ladd happily, as his face froze in what I'd call "sickened horror."

He didn't even say goodbye.

The People Love Loud

The Pond was filled with humanity. American humanity. Sold-out American humanity. Many of the excited American humans were pre-teen or what futurist Faith Popcorn no doubt calls "tweens." Also, there were five gay guys; they were very shiny and wholesome, like all America's favorite gays. The tweens were screaming. Actually *screaming* does it about as much justice as calling pundit provocateur Ann Coulter mildly disagreeable. In fact, the pre-teen and tween Americans were shrieking and wailing and carrying on like they'd been transported back to a 1984 Wham! show or something. Whatev!

"It's like running into someone you know at a gay bar," my boyfriend hoped as we bought some scalped tickets outside from the best scalper ever (he sold us a pair for less than face value and they weren't even fake!). "They can't bust you because *you* saw *them* there, too!"

"Yeah. Unless they're here because they brought their kids," I reminded him, my usual bucket-of-ice-water-on-his-hopes-and-dreams self. His hopes were dashed. There were a shocking number of Americans present without children to justify their choice of Sunday night entertainment—at $25 to $50 a pop—and we were among them. If anybody saw us, we had no starry-eyed and runny-nosed excuse whatsoever for being two out of 16,000 fans at the American Idol Tour Sunday night. *Eeeeeeeeeeeeeeeeeeeeeeeeeeeeeee!!!!!!!!!!*

So how do you make fun of an American Idol concert without being a big, 909-bashing elitist class snob, sneering at the rubes and yokels? How do you deplore the fact that people scarf down whatever Fox tells them to swallow—down to the most depressing product placement—without condescendingly implying that they're tasteless hicks who aren't as good as those of us who live in *the city* and go to concerts by actual bands? Christ, who wants to play hipper-than-thou? And would it be wrong to mention that a lot of people were grossly fat? I mean, that's a real problem in this country! And how do you gently chide the old white people who were *crying* during Clay Aiken's boring ballad—which was so boring I couldn't even be bothered to write down what song it was, because I was benumbed—without falling into the dismaying trap of mean and nasty class warfare? I find jokes about trailer trash appalling; poor whites and Southerners are the last people we're permitted to jeer at as a group, and I think it's awful. But what am I supposed to do? *Not* make fun of the twinkly young superstar who batted his eyelashes from the ginormous screen like he was Liberace? And neglect to tell you that some of the families that hadn't brought children but were singing and crying anyway looked a little bit like competitors in the Special Olympics? And that they were fat?

As a matter of fact, the Pond was a little piece of heaven, even if (sadly) the inane and gilded host of the TV show, Ryan Seacrest, was not there to ramble on about his hair. We watched in awe as girls in matching, home-made, lime Ruben shirts positively *sashayed* through the halls, their hips svelte and their legs coltish. They were outnumbered twenty to one, easy, by grown-up old white people sporting preprinted red Clay shirts. We hoped there wouldn't be trouble between the competing boy-love factions. Maybe a dance-off, like in "Beat It"? The Ruben girls, slim and multiethnic, would tap-dance on the old white people's fat, diabetic corpses in any kind of matchup. It wouldn't be pretty—race riots so rarely are. But rhythmic? Yes, it would be that.

The show had yet to start, and plain, bespectacled middle-aged women were herding large groups of teenage girls into something resembling order. Very, very loud order. It was very touching, all the good moms there, game and actually enjoying the twaddle. One mom-type lady was holding a banner. *Clay,* it read, *These Girls Are Yours.* It was kinda funny, the unintended paternity-suit quality of the language, except her own dormant sexuality was the last thing on her mind. Rather, she was offering to turn out any of the Ashleys, Brittanys and Caitlyns in her charge. At what point do you decide it's time to draw the attention of a doubtless deviant pop star to your Girl Scout troop?

And would she have raised the same banner at an R. Kelly show, or is Clay just totally non-threateningly gay?

We got an excellent margarita and a not at all bad turkey sandwich (though if they're going to go to the trouble of making it right there when you order it, couldn't they throw in some tomato, lettuce and cheese as well?), and we settled in, watching the commercials on the huge screen. Girls screamed. People were happy. It was happy time. Really, for reals, it was *feliz*. We were part of something—something a small bit teenybop, perhaps, but something. You don't sneeze at a 16,000-person scream; you let yourself be caught up in the communal emotion, the mass hysteria, the mob mentality, even if your boyfriend *is* embarrassed by you—and he is. A Latino dude was next to us. Could he explain to us why the girls were screaming at the video screen showing commercials for Pop-Tarts, which was sponsoring the tour (and which one of the *American Idol* finalists would go on to *thank*)? "You'll have to ask my son," our neighbor declaimed; he was laughing and friendly, but he scrunched down in his seat, wanting to be sure we knew he was suffering through this for the kid's sake. We understood *completely*.

The ladies behind us did not suffer. They had multigenerational mullets, from mid-twenties and hefty to early-fifties and transported. Later, they would stand and bounce, singing all the words to all the songs, with shiny eyes.

And then, after some more commercials, it was time for the concert to begin!!! *Eeeeeeeeeeeeeeeeeeeeeeeeeeeeeee! !!!!!!!!!!!!!!!!*

The people loved Clay loudest. I don't know why, for Ruben was equally boring. And for some reason, Clay got to own the color red, just like Mao! All the Clay shirts were red, and people shone red lights during his dull, dull song, where he stood motionless at the mic stand until about three-quarters through it, and by the simple act of finally walking away from the spot where he'd been standing, made every girl in the place go insane with shrieking. *All he did was walk to one side of the stage, and everybody screamed.* Everybody else had to at least pretend to dance, even the fat black dudes (who wheezed), but all the white boy (emoting jovially like Ronald Reagan telling an especially inane anecdote) had to do was walk, and he got ten times the love and panties. He had really expensive highlights, Ryan Seacrest-style.

Some of the performers—okay, pretty much one young woman named Trenyce—were terrific. (Also, the slutty blonde one— "Kimberly," I think— had a pleasant voice, low and throaty like Fiona Apple's lower register.) And there were even some pyrotechnics during Trenyce's damn rocking cover of the Tina Turner version of "Proud Mary." Also, Trenyce had freakishly large hands; they were as big as Gerald Ford's noggin. They were like Cubist hands, and they were cool.

And, sweetly, after each performer, they brought up the houselights so Julia and Kimberly would be able to see the plethora of homemade signs emblazoned with their names. How heartbreaking would it be to make a sign, and then not have, um, Carmen or Charlie be able to read it in the dark? It would be very heartbreaking!

Now, I understand *American Idol* was quite popular, and people seemed to like it very well. Hell, lots of them even paid $25 to $50 to go hear *American Idol* finalists sing one cover song each before introducing the next *American Idol* finalist and thanking the fans—who made it possible!—and Pop-Tarts. That's awfully big money for a karaoke show!

It's a karaoke show with backup dancers, sure—they came out first in "street kid" costumes, busting those moves by that Nsync choreographer, the one whose video I could have gotten at the As Seen On TV store at The Block, but I got *Back Yard Fight Clubs* instead, and I'm still mad about it even though that was last Christmas.

Yeah, so the backup dancers were fine—although the pretty black dancer with the fabulous Afro was later, during Rickey Smith's song, supposed to be that girl that Michael Jackson stalks in the video for "The Way You Make Me Feel," a song I actually really like. She strutted around confusedly as Smith pretty much ignored her; also, he had a kind of bad Mike Tyson voice, so she was pretty much left to get stalked by a lady man who had as much interest in stalking her as Michael Jackson had in the original. (And by the way, did the video director all those years ago not get the memo about rape and how by the nineties it had lost some of its sexy?)

Where was I?

Oh, yes. Rape is bad.

But it did make me happy—the show, not rape—and it was nice, and the little girls got their first taste of hot lust even though their moms still shouldn't let them dress like that, and the rest of us got our bread and circuses and an hour or two of joy and screeches for Labor Day. We hope you had a happy one.

my Liev as a Dog

So there I was at Heather Graham's birthday party Friday night. I had tagged along with someone who'd tagged along with someone who'd tagged along with the DJ. That's right, people: I was just three degrees of separation from the help!

Well, there we are, waiting outside Tokio on Cahuenga Boulevard because it's jammed inside the tiny club, Ted Danson and Mary Steenburgen are chilling on the sidewalk, and up walks *Liev Schreiber*!

Who? you ask. Because, really, he's not that famous.

Okay. He was in *The Daytrippers*? Where he played Parker Posey's boyfriend who wrote the hilarious novel? No? Okay. He was the ex-boyfriend in the Meg Ryan time-travel romance *Kate & Leopold*? No? Well, he's not that famous.

Still, he's one of the few (maybe half a dozen) actors I would freak out to see in person because he's so tall and Jewish and droopily handsome, and I even know how to pronounce his first name (rhymes with Kiev), and his parts are so witty and intelligent! (The Orson Welles biopic *RKO 281*? No? Okay.) He's so intelligent, in fact, that if you web-stalk him, you'll come up with this quote from the Yale website: "[Yale] had a huge effect on my life and my career as well," he said at some pooterific Yale shindig. "Yale has solidified my love of text."

See? Liev Schreiber "loves text"!

Now, we'd already been at a small cocktail get-together, poolside at the Avalon Hotel, for novelist, *Vanity Fair* guy and bona fide Commie Girl-pal Neal Pollack, who was in town pitching to the movie folk (and who got *Vanity Fair* to pay for it; clever Neal Pollack!). At this cocktail thing, we listened to girl agents talk about their $240 pants and say things like, "Well, you know, if I just need staples and I want to go cheap, then I'll go to Banana Republic." And then we listened to this woman talk about how Maya Lin (you remember Maya Lin from such projects as, oh, the Vietnam Veterans Memorial) was redesigning her *house*. We decided the girl agents were probably less lethal. But then a weird thing happened! After the girl agents left to go to their pole-dancing aerobics class, we talked more to the woman with the house, and she turned out to be supercool and not nearly as pretentious as the conversation had at first suggested, and she was actually groovy and kind of reckless too, and she invited us to go to Heather Graham's party with her because she knew the DJ! So that's why we were sitting there on Cahuenga Boulevard, waiting to get into Tokio, but not for terribly long: someone who promised to get us into a party, it turned out, could actually get us into a party.

So up walks Liev Schreiber! (Who?) And I'm freaking out, and I decide it's time to grow some balls and go say something clever and hopefully charming. He's outside because he can't get into the party (because, really, he's not that famous), and his back is to me when I walk up and gently touch his shoulder and say, softly, "Excuse me." That's when he turns farther away.

Maybe he didn't hear me. I slink back into line.

We get into the party a solid twenty minutes before he does because, really, he's not that famous, and we're having a fabulous free-drinky time in the soup of sweat coming from the dance floor. Well, finally Liev Schreiber gets into the party, and I decide to stalk him once more. He's not there with a date; he's not trying to finish a meal in peace for once, god damn it, just once; I am not waving a camera lens in his face; and we are guests at the same private party, even if I am tagging along with the help.

He's talking in a desultory manner—he looks bored, actually—with some guy he knows, and I go stand at his elbow, waiting for a break in the conversation so as not to interrupt. I stand there, the smile pinned to my face becoming less and less natural and buoyant, for five minutes. Maybe seven. Far too long. And there's no way to extricate myself gracefully from this situation because I have fearlessly stated with my presence that I have come over to say something clever and charming—something like "Hello!"—and he has clearly stated his intention to refuse to look down in the region of his right elbow and smile or nod or acknowledge in any way that I am a person standing there waiting to say something to him—I'm not important, pretty or good enough even to nod to.

I'm sure I've been more embarrassed but never when it didn't involve accidental public nudity or an ill-timed vomit.

A tip for you, Liev Schreiber: way more famous people than you have *also* not wanted to talk to me. They do anyway. Because we're people, we smile. We nod. We exchange a sentence or two even if it's just "It's inappropriate for you to follow me to my home," or "Stop hitting me, Liza!" And then we graciously excuse ourself if need be. It's perfectly acceptable, and it's what people do. Think of all you miss—like my "text." If I had been all snobby and horrible and cold and cadaverous and incapable of human emotion, like you, I wouldn't have had any fun at Laguna Beach's Marine Room the next night. I would have shut myself off with a scowl from talking and dancing with the two 23-year-old, six-foot-three Marines trying to buy me birthday drinks (and succeeding—darlings, semper fi!). And I couldn't have danced joyously to the band at the Sandpiper, aka the Dirty Bird, who were pleasing me with their poppy Oasis and Squeeze (and the singer had a funny constipated intensity) until my sister decided she wasn't having a heavy-metal enough time, and we had to leave. I would have no friends with whom to wander the night, no human contact whatsoever. Oh, well. You'll always have text.

SECTION TWO

God Is Love

The Church Of Phil

Crooner Phil Shane just wants the world to love him. With his wife, Michlene, he's gotten off to a good start. And now, with a Vegas tryout, all his dreams may come true

Phil Shane is ministering to the lovesick, the aged, the hip and the drunk. From atop his high stage, he bends down for the laying-on of hands: in this case, a slow, tender kiss (sans tongue) for a giggling blonde who pretends to faint and then snatches his long white scarf as a pilgrim's relic.

The Celebration Lounge at Las Vegas' Tropicana Hotel and Casino is spacious, with high ceilings accented in copper and teal. Low, comfortable bucket chairs in what seems to be black pleather surround tiny tables littered with the remains of margaritas. The stage is roomy enough for his rack of sequined jackets, which he swaps according to his mood or song list.

This is neither Santa Ana's crusty Fling—equal parts groping seventy-year-olds and pierced kids, where Shane sings from behind and sometimes atop the C-shaped piano bar—nor Dana Point's graying and wealthy Harpoon Henry's. It is not Fullerton's slightly creepy 2J's—a fun dive with just a whiff of speed freak—or the crowded, literally underground La Cave. It is none of the OC spots at which Shane has been gigging since 1972. Thirty years. And after thirty years, this, baby, is *Vegas*, even if his slot is in the middle of the afternoon.

At 5 p.m., the small crowd is still slumped in its seats. To our right is a quartet of cute folk in their very early twenties, possibly even late teens. The girls are pretty if not flashy, and their companions are dorky Midwestern guys. All are sullen for a while. But soon they understand the program: Shane will sing every song they throw at him, smiling like Stevie Wonder all the while. And if he doesn't have the request on the minidiscs he switches during the set—this is professional karaoke, hon—then he will pick up his guitar and play it. "Copacabana"? Certainly! A little Creedence? He'll get on it next! Right now, he's gonna do a little Tom Jones. Are there any Tom Jones fans here tonight? He leads us through "Delilah" and "What's New, Pussycat?" Like Jones's, Shane's black pants are so tight that if he were a woman, he'd be sporting a cameltoe. I didn't think that in this environment, he'd come so close to touching his unit, but indeed his hand is mere millimeters away. Aw, yeah!

Shane will work so hard tonight, taking no breaks, pouring gallons of sweat and affixing a smile to his face every second he's onstage—but it's never, ever fake. Indeed, he would work equally hard if there were only three tables full. All he wants, God willing, is for people to enjoy themselves and have a little party. He just wants to be loved.

By 6 p.m., to the rollicking strains of John Cougar Mellencamp's "Hurts So Good," the girls talk the boys into dancing: though goofy, the boys try their best, undulating clumpily while the girls shake their buns with sexy grace. Later, two much cockier young men in caps and baggy jeans (they look like Irvine guys trying to be Huntington Beach thugs but unwilling to commit to the tattoos) will come and hover over the girls until the Iowans are banished. Vegas is a soap opera, and we are glued to it.

But when Shane puts on his white, studded Elvis jacket and silly, big sunglasses, the interlopers have not yet appeared. Iowa is still happily in the game, and the quartet whoops and hollers.

A break is enforced at 7:30 p.m. so that a big spin of big prizes can commence. Shane, as any of his Orange County fans will attest, does not *take* breaks, but this is Vegas, and he's not going to make waves. The spin is lame: nobody wins the $1,000 top prize or even the $100 prize. Instead, each of the spinners is granted dinner at Calypso's (the Trop's coffee shop) or tickets to Rick Thomas, who, judging by his publicity still, is a lonely knock-off of big-haired tiger tamers Siegfried and Roy in the days before their act came to an abrupt, and unscheduled, end. A lovely showgirl with a face straight out of 1934 (Clara Bow lips and porcelain beauty) points to stuff, her gut sucked in every second of her shift. Her teal thong looks terribly uncomfortable to the feminine eye, but the men in my party are oblivious to her pain. They are cruel and demanding in their love.

Every Tuesday through Saturday Shane's set begins at 3 p.m.—an uncivilized hour in Las Vegas, Nevada—and ends by 8:20 p.m. The Trop management actually wanted him to do sets that ran slightly shy of an hour, with breaks in between. But Phil Shane does not do that to his fans. And by 8:20 p.m., *everyone* is a fan: old, mean Danish ladies will be stealing any seat that's left unattended for even a moment.

In his silly glasses, grinning like a moron, Shane sings the Elvis classic "Love Me." I climb onto my date's lap and sprawl there, overcome. The quartet are no longer wry, laconic sneerers. They sway, enthralled and touched. They understand now. They get it. They have joined the Church of Phil. And watching over it all, enthroned at a table surrounded by Orange County friends and gazing at him with an omnipresent shy smile, is Phil's wife of eight years, Michlene. Love him? Oh, she does!

Treat me like a fool/Treat me mean and cruel/But love me/Wring my faithful heart/Tear it all apart/But love me.

Phil Shane was born in Tupelo, Mississippi, in 1949. On the stage, he looks like a young-hearted forty-four, but as soon as he steps off it, his age shows. It's uncanny: the distance is the same, but all of a sudden, he's fifty-two and *really* sweaty. He has never held another job. Not waiter or dogwalker. From the age of thirteen, he has made his living playing in the band.

Until the mid-sixties, Mississippi was a dry state. But Tupelo's sheriff had a supper club outside town: the Chicksa Lodge. Jerry Lee Lewis played there. Singers came from Nashville and Alabama, even Florida. And from the time he was thirteen, Shane played there, too. Back then, he was on bass; the karaoke machine had yet to be invented.

"This is kind of personal," Shane says in his low, rich Southern voice, but he doesn't say the magic words "off the record." "My dad had a terrible gambling problem, and he actually lost our house in a game of dominoes. My mom left him that same day. I think I got out with my clothes and my record player."

For this reason, when I take him to shoot craps later in the evening, Shane has no idea how the game works. He simply doesn't gamble.

His mother was a bookkeeper for a dry cleaner, and though they were never lacking in food or shelter, making ends meet even in Mississippi was hard to do. The money Shane's gigging brought in helped immeasurably. Still, his mother's brother, a minister, made Shane's immorality the subject of his sermon one Sunday. He called him out by name, said Phil was going straight to hell, working as he was in a place rife with booze and loose women. Shane still hasn't gotten over the embarrassment and the injustice of it.

"He knew I was helping my mom out," he says. "He knew my dad wasn't there."

He married young, a next-door neighbor, and together they moved to Orange County in the early seventies. Why OC? It's where Disneyland was.

Shane and his wife lived in an RV parked out behind Reagan's (now Patsy's), a Mission Viejo bar where they sang.

And then, in 1988, Michlene came into the picture. Michlene was the mother of nine-year-old twins, and her husband had passed away. She was stunned by Phil's talent, and she "tried really hard to like his wife, too," she says. But he was married, and though she had very strong feelings for him, Michlene decided she had been put into his life for another purpose. She would be his manager. She would serve his talent. She would make him go places, no matter how many obstacles he came up with.

"It's 'I-can't-because,'" says Michlene, sounding as dismissive as her sweet voice can. "'I-can't-because.' I don't want to hear, 'I-can't-because.' I asked Phil, 'What do *you want* to do?' and he said he wanted to play the Dana Point Harbor, but he couldn't because . . . Well, I got him into the harbor and asked, 'What do you want to do now?'" Eventually, Phil was sneaking into Michlene's bedroom window. In '92, he moved in. He divorced his wife, and in '94, Phil and Michlene married.

Now I'll say it: Michlene and Phil look positively bizarre together. Phil is five-foot-three (and a half), and has a puffy Neil Diamond pompadour that on a good day takes ten minutes to blow-dry and on a bad day . . . "You don't want to be in the same house on a bad day!" says Michlene.

Michlene is five-foot-eight (and a half), and to speak plainly, she's a lot of woman. Her dark hair is gelled and country-big. Her nails are long and red. Her stunning blue eyes are thickly lined; it's easy to get lost in them. In fact, she resembles Elizabeth Taylor. But however mismatched they may at first appear, their devotion is so palpable it can incite a melancholy envy.

There she sits in the back with her friends. Does she go to all his shows? "He likes to have me with him," she says softly. And now she is with him in Vegas, skipping home on Mondays and Tuesdays to check her PO box—she's a theatrical manager for performing twins with her business, Carbon Copies— and then heading back to the bright lights of the Celebration.

Ten years ago, she wouldn't have been able to, but heck, she's got a cell phone; she can conduct her business wherever she is. Before every show, she sews four white scarves for him to hand out to other ladies. She makes fans from construction paper, a cartoon Phil photocopied on each one. After Phil's set, you will see Michlene helping him transport his many jackets. If they were home in OC, they would cap off the evening in their aquamarine and redwood hot tub. "It's our favorite thing ever!" Michlene says. And what does she love most about him? She thinks for a moment. "His passion for everything that he loves," she says, and she pulls herself up to her full height and speaks with quiet pride. "Including me."

Phil Shane is making his long-overdue Vegas debut because Michlene made it happen. There was no "I-can't-because." So now the glittering Tropicana is giving him an extended tryout, running through May 5. Michlene, ever the optimist and businesswoman, has signed a six-month lease on an apartment there.

"It's only $469 per month, and it's a write-off!" she says. "Even if he doesn't get it, well, we'll have a place to stay when we come here for the weekend!" Of course, not for a second does she believe he won't be offered the job. She doesn't believe in won'ts. I ask Phil what he loves most about Michlene.

"She's the most positive person I've ever met in my life," he says. "If she has a negative thought, she just throws it right out."

If Phil belongs in Vegas—and he does—she will see to it. She will make it happen. And they will be together, preferably in a hot tub.

The same positivity Michlene brings to the business end of Phil's career, he delivers to the audience. Let's face it: the act is dorky. He sings Neil Diamond and "God Bless the USA," backed up not by a band but by a machine. His outfits are full of sequins. He's really short. But as God is my witness, the love he projects from that stage is given back to him a thousandfold. I ask him if he's ever had a bad show. "Well, sure, I guess," he says. "When I was sick."

He once played a New Year's Eve show with strep throat; his doctor assured him that though it would be painful, it wouldn't damage his vocal cords. And he sang through the pain, caring only that the audience had a good time. "I didn't want people to know I was feeling bad," he says. "I wanted it to be a party!"

The people of Orange County have felt the love. Debbie Bartz, a Shane friend for twenty-five years, is the president of his fan club, which boasts thirty-five or forty members (the $5 dues cover postage for the photo and newsletter). Two years ago, she got his face tattooed on her back. "It started out as a dare," she says, "but then I thought, I've known him and loved him for a long time." A few years ago, when Debbie's daughter got married, it was Phil Shane who gave away the bride.

Shane's been playing to the bluehairs at Harpoon Henry's for quite a while, as well as, for four years now, to the seedier variety of bluehair that inhabits the Fling. But it was Robert Williams, lead singer of the beloved roots band Big Sandy who was responsible for introducing him to the scenesters who adore him so persistently now.

"It was at Big Sandy's Christmas party that all the kids saw me for the first time, I think," Shane tells me. "Weren't you at that party?" In fact, I was. That was in 1998, and until this Vegas trip, Shane and I have never so much as said hello, but he remembers nonetheless.

"That's the thing," Robert says. "When you walk in, he takes a minute and looks up and smiles. He's so happy to see you. Even when he doesn't know you, he makes you feel like a personal friend." Robert pauses, trying to find the right words. "You can tell he truly just loves what he's doing. I've gone to see other lounge singers . . ." He trails off. What he means is that some lounge singers are hacks. And Phil Shane is not. He smiles every second he's onstage because he's in love every second he's there. I ask Michlene if he's always like that.

"Oh, he gets moody!" she assures me. "But never when he's onstage. I want to build him a stage in the house, and whenever he gets grumpy, I'll tell him, 'Go get on that stage! Right now!'"

Back at the Tropicana on this Saturday night, we yell out from the crowd for "I'm a Believer." "Oh, that's a great one!" says Shane happily. "Neil Diamond wrote this one, recorded by the Monkees. I don't have it on disc, but I'll play it for you!" He picks up his guitar, slings it over his shoulder, and starts strumming wildly. He looks up toward heaven—or, in the Tropicana's case, toward the gilded ceiling—and I swear his face is lit with a heavenly glow. At that moment, we are all believers. We all ache for love.

real live boys

I was nice on Saturday—I usually am, in person. I didn't tell a single person I met that I wished their children had never been born.

You kind of expect The Children of the Corn when you hang out with the Snowflakes—the formerly frozen embryos who've been saved from spending eternity in a Petri dish by a load of adoptifyin' Jesus freaks. They're not *AI* robot zombies at all: they're as apple-cheeked and bouncy as any real child. Really, they're lovely, and I hate them nonetheless.

For decades it's been a truism that those on the Right only love you till you're born, and then you've got a freaking bull's eye on your head.

But it's never been truer than today: on a new front in the abortion wars, the Right is encouraging adoption of *embryos*—that's eight cells each, y'all— and encouraging the adopters to apply for a $10,000 federal tax credit, while they're at it. That's the tax credit that's meant to help out folks who take in post-born homeless waifs—and how it got twisted to include infertile couples helping themselves to some donated eggs while singing choruses of hallelujahs to their own beneficence I haven't the faintest idea. My money's on Kansas Senator Sam Brownback. He's a real prick.

Saturday, on a beautiful afternoon at Irvine Regional Park, I attended a barbecue for those sweet little Snowflakes. There are more than one hundred of them so far—and twenty in the oven who'll be ready by March. Of course, there are more than 400,000 frozen embryos that are discarded by the yuppies who can't have kids without a little help from the men in the lab coats.

The pro-life crowd can't call in vitro fertilization "murder," of course— just like they can't advocate that women who get abortions go to jail—despite the number of embryos left in limbo. But they can call stem cell research from those embryos murder. You all remember, I'm sure, that during El Prez's nauseating speech about stem cell research, explaining why after six years in office he was finally breaking out his veto pen, he was surrounded by little beauties—true beauties—who had been adopted from frozen embryos. But they weren't little frozen things: the Blue Fairy came down and made them real live children.

So *this* is the Right's new focus? Saving embryos comprising eight cells each? People can disagree on abortion—hell, I disagree with *myself* on abortion—but eight cells? You'll make *them* your cause when there are more than 100,000 foster children in California alone who are dying for a permanent family, and 5 million children in California who live in poverty?

Meanwhile, those on the Right who moon on and on about the rights of the unborn are the same people you will hear describe welfare to help little poor children whose mothers *didn't* abort them as "the transfer of wealth through force and coercion," or, more simply, "theft." Reducing unwanted pregnancies in the first place, through sex education and readily available family planning services? "Immoral." (The most cuckoo among them even think the Pill is murder—and will call my radio show to tell me so—because it doesn't let the egg get fertilized in the first place. If that means we have to start burying our Tampax in consecrated ground, so be it.) Lobbying against the FDA approving a vaccine for the human papilloma virus (better known to many of us as Our Friend the Genital Wart) even though HPV is responsible for 250,000 cervical cancer deaths a year, because curing the disease would "encourage promiscuity among young women"? I've had just about enough of the "pro-life."

If people who had Snowflake children just said, "Yes, we really wanted a baby and couldn't have one on our own, but luckily a nice lady with extras donated an egg," I wouldn't be making any hay here. I'm not personally a fan of IVF—if people who *can't* bear children don't adopt, that really screws up the invisible hand of the homeless-waif marketplace—but people do their things and make their choices, and to some people (some people who are assholes) having a kid from your vagina is the most important thing.

It's the sanctimonious *cause*, the saving of these cells when there are actual post-embryo children who'd sure like to be saved (and the sanctimonious plucking of that lovely tax credit), that makes me fucking crazy.

I listened while the speaker introducing Congressman Ed Royce thanked him for working on behalf of "those of us who have *values*"—his emphasis— and I listened as Hannah's mom told the crowd, "She knows she's adopted, and knows she, mommy and daddy were all adopted into God's family because Christ died on the cross." I listened to one person say, "We have to be defenders of *life*," and I listened as another mother said, of her desire to have children, "God said, 'No. It's a good plan, but it's not My plan.' So we prayed about it and prayed about it, and then we heard about Snowflakes, and we said, 'We think we need to try this and see what God does.'" Honey, that ain't God. That's Repronex and Gonal-f. God had already answered you, remember?

a simple story

Trish had been on the waiting list for five years. They'd told her it would be two. And once she got to the front of the list, she had sixty days. If she couldn't find an apartment that would take her Section 8 housing voucher in that time, back to the end of the list she and her baby would go.

I never asked Trish what she had done to get herself homeless and sleeping on the floor of the Santa Ana Catholic Worker. I really didn't care.

Trish isn't mentally handicapped, or a drug addict. She's a little weatherbeaten, but when she starts talking, she could be anyone you know. When she was pregnant with her son five years ago, his dad had "legal problems." The Catholic Worker took her in. Get on CalWorks, the good lefties said, and the housing list. She did. She left for a while, stayed in motels and on the floors of family members. She's been back now a full year, sleeping in the backyard of the big house on Cypress Street.

Trish is one of the lucky ones: able to understand and fight through the red tape of the county, state and federal welfare agencies' regulations. She had twelve days left (of the sixty permitted), when, after visiting the agencies every morning to find new housing listings, and finding that every one of the listings was for senior housing, or no longer took Section 8, or had already been rented, or wanted copies of her driver's license, Social, tax returns for two years, check stubs for six months, and a $35 fee for a credit check (when it's supposed by law to be $20), not to mention all those $200 nonrefundable deposits, and then rented out the place to someone who wasn't on Section 8 anyway, well, Trish actually found a place. A fireman from Cypress had bought and gutted some places, and she was the first person who called. For $950 a month from this nation of ours, Trish and her son will have a bed and a bath, a common washer and dryer, and new and shiny everything.

"It used to be a drug neighborhood," she says, "but it's been built up."

It's tiny, she says, but beautiful.

While she talks to me, her son plays with a woman, twenty-five, black and profoundly retarded. "They adopted each other," Trish says.

Trish and I talk a long time, sitting on a bench in the yard where later people will sleep. There are hundreds of them, in a place of last resort. "I see their faces, that shell-shocked look, and their kids clinging to them. It's hard for new families," she says. They put the new ones and the ones with the littlest kids inside to bunk on the floor; they make room for the newest ones by moving outdoors. County shelters run only December to April; the Rescue Mission is for men only; at the Salvation Army you can stay for only a week per month. So the cops and the hospitals bring people here. When a nine-months-pregnant battered woman tried the pregnancy shelters, none would take her because she was too close to her due date. Dwight and Leia Smith, who opened this outpost of the Catholic Worker a decade ago, were there.

On the front porch, the kids are getting once-a-week tutoring from various do-gooding libs. "I like houses because I want one," a kid writes.

Twice a week, a guy brings his music students down from Pico Rivera to give lessons. The kids in that program marched at Disneyland. Eight of the children are going to Carnegie Hall—practice practice practice—while the Pico Rivera school raises money for the trip.

After the kids go back to their parents and the tutors go home, Leia stands out on her big front porch. She laughs and chats; she loves this life. She says, "I made a wish on my twenty-first birthday that when I was fifty, my life wouldn't be boring." And with the constant adrenalin and drama of bringing everyone who needs you into your life and your home, I guess it never has been. She talks about dignity, family values and the Culture of Life.

It's probably not the Culture of Life you've heard much about.

Those Culture of Lifers—the dominant kind in our county—are the people who talk about welfare as "theft." The ones who weep for your baby till the moment he's born. They natter on and on with their self-satisfied ideas about all kinds of things, but mostly thundering denunciations of taxes. It's coercive and Marxist, they say, to transfer wealth. Of course, there was welfare in colonial Massachusetts, predating Marx and Engels by a good little bit, because men have always left their wives or flat gone off and died. At the same time that the Right's grand apologia for economic hardship—Schumpeter's notion of "Creative Destruction"—allows that sometimes people won't be able to get jobs because economies must destroy themselves to grow, the flip side of that (helping out those destroyed by these vibrant economic changes) is *un-American*. It's all about personal responsibility and rugged individualism, they tell me—when they've never had to worry a moment in their lives.

Trish and her son will go to sleep tonight on a picnic table in a Santa Ana backyard. She's a lucky one: she'll have a tiny and beautiful apartment soon, from which she can go to her classes to become an ultrasound tech. The taxpayers will pay $950 a month for it. I can't imagine we could spend it on anything better.

itching With it

It's all so retarded, I'm positively itching with it. I think the War on Christmas gave me the crabs.

There's Bill O'Reilly and the Catholic League's loopy William Donohue, of course. There's also Worldview Weekend, the tender website with the world's best Bible quiz, which says the most biblical way to assess taxes is through the very very rich Steve Forbes' flat tax—which I'm pretty sure would be news to Jesus—but I swear I just read it for the articles by onetime teen-TV heartthrob Kirk Cameron of *Growing Pains* and, apparently, the Left Behind movies. We got each other! Sharing the laughter and love! Until our one and only lord and savior comes down and shoots unbelievers with machine-gun bullets from the wounds in his palms. Hey, remember that Very Special Episode when Kirk Cameron lost his virginity? Yeah, me either. But Christopher Cross did the theme song for that episode, and then I saw him play it at Garden Grove's community concert, and he introduced it all (and he was totally pompous), "I did this song for a Very Special Episode of *Growing Pains* when Kirk Cameron lost his virginity." It was a stupid song, and after the show I asked him why he hadn't played the theme from *Greatest American Hero*, and it turned out it was because that wasn't his song. Didn't you think it was? Me too! Christopher Cross seemed kind of miffed.

Anyway, they're all bitching and crying their big fat victim tears about how *oppressed* they are every time someone says "Happy Holidays" as a way to maybe include season's greetings of peace and joy (unto you!) to those in our big, wonderful melting pot who maybe don't believe in Jesus. At least, they don't believe in Jesus now, but that'll all get cleared up as soon as Tom DeLay's

Dominionists have their way, at which time America shall have forced conversions and live by "biblical principles."

You know what I miss? Stoning.

I wished my aunt a Merry Christmas last week; she's one of those militant Jews who goes to temple and writes checks to Planned Parenthood and the ACLU. Even though she and my dad celebrated Christmas as kids (read Philip Roth's *The Plot Against America*: Newark Jews, as OC's own much-missed bigamist Bircher Congressman John Schmitz used to say, were just like everyone else, only more so), she totally doesn't now! It's all Hanukkah this, and Passover that, when Christmas and Easter are perfectly good seasonal substitutes for holidays that are pretty much seasonal substitutes themselves for winter and spring solstice celebrations by the hell-bound idolists, and they'll have much less chance of Torquemada finding out. I don't think she thought it was funny, but then the only time I've seen her laugh *really* hard was at Jackie Mason's one-man Broadway show when he was talking about how Jews can't program their VCRs. Jews can really be sensitive, but apparently anything Jackie Mason said was comedy gold!

But all that mockery of the War on Christmas—and of O'Reilly, who said he was going to "bring horror" to the perpetrators, a phrase I think I last heard come out of Osama's mouth—was before I agreed to be a judge in South Coast Plaza's window-display contest in exchange for a sweet $25 gift certificate and all the champagne my little system could carry. Plus, it got me out of the office on a Tuesday night, the night of the week when my small buttercup of a son has to sit with me in the office till sometimes 9:30 p.m. while I proof the final layout of the paper just so I can prove to everybody what a goddamn team player I am. And it was in the shining lights of SCP, basking in the tones of the pure, sweet soprano quartet The Sleigh Belles and surrounded by the lovely scents of seared ahi tuna and money, that I discovered: there really is a War on Christmas. Of course, it's nothing like the one our Founding Fathers waged; they'd fine your ass in Puritan Massachusetts for celebrating it. But I'm sure you knew that already . . .

Of the ten windows I was assigned to judge, maybe four had no Christmas decorations at all. Maybe four more decorated for the season in festive shades of iron gray. One store had a window done up in sheaths of wheat, which looked cool for an autumn equinox window-judging competition, if you're a *freaking pagan*! And Versace wasn't specifically Christmasy in the slightest, but the mannequins looked like they were at a really fun party. I would like to go to that party! You win, Versace, damn you! *You win.*

everyone Has aiDS! [aiDS aiDS aiDS aiDS aiDS, aiDS!]

According to *Team America: World Police*, everyone has AIDS. My father (AIDS!). My sister (AIDS!). The gays and the straights and the whites and the spades.

AIDS!

Actually, in my family, everyone has Hep C. (It must have been all those prison stints.) But we have AIDS too, or we did; my son's first mom (my stepmother) died of it when he was a baby.

So did I go to Friday's Global Summit on AIDS at Saddleback Church in some kind of activist solidarity? Because this time, it's personal? No, not really. Eleven years later, I don't think about Leslie that often—except sometimes to mumble an apology to her when I've been particularly menstrual and rotten to her sweet son, and to promise her I really am taking good care of him, mostly.

Really, I just went to see Senator Barack Obama address Rick Warren's megachurch, and to find out how the holy rollers would welcome him.

Quite well, as it turned out. If nothing else, they're a very welcoming lot.

All those e-mails I got from the Worldview Weekend nutso types promising hellfire for Obama's positions on abortion and gay marriage (he's actually, and very uncoolly, against gay marriage, but not according to the good reverends at Worldview)? Well, they managed to find two sad people willing to protest the gathering, down miles of winding driveway where the Saddleback "campus" meets the street. "Stop AIDS," read their signs. "Stop sin." I stopped myself from giving them the finger, and just glared at them instead. I hope Miss Manners realizes how highly I rate her etiquette advice.

Rick Warren, who started the seminal megachurch Saddleback with his wife, Kay, twenty-six years ago, was getting ready to testify when I arrived. White people were clapping choppily to a kind of actually rocking band. For serious! My lip was twitching. Do. Not. Laugh!

Jew!

I was greeted by multiple greeters—right on its website, Saddleback promises you will always be greeted, and that's one promise they kept. But it's nice, being smiled at and given a good morning; it's like Wal-Mart, except people are there because they want to be, not forced to work—at Wal-Mart—despite their arthritis and general anciency.

Also unlike Wal-Mart, the space (chapel? meeting hall? coven?) is modern and airy, with exposed white pipes and easily a hundred grand in stage lights.

Warren talked a long time—he's a talker, that Rick Warren—and he looked like an older version of my brother-in-law, with his goatee and jeans and general puffiness. But Rick Warren is an interesting guy. He may look like your typical white OC kind of . . . you know . . . asshole. But he was talking about how he never realized AIDS was a problem until Kay made him look at the situation in Africa, where 12 million orphans wander the streets, their parents dead of AIDS.

"That," he said, "is a continent sliding into the sea."

So what else had he missed? He made a list of the world's most pressing problems, the ones governments couldn't or wouldn't fix. Why couldn't he, Rick Warren, focus the energies of his 12,000 parishioners (are they called parishioners?) to fight spiritual emptiness, "egocentric leadership" (or corruption— "There are little Saddams in every country, in every community, in every church and in every homeowners' association," he said. "Give a man a little power, he turns into Stalin."), poverty, pandemic diseases and illiteracy?

"My goal," he said, "is to turn the American church from selfish consumerism to selfless contribution. I want to see a woman, who was once only interested in her diamond tennis bracelet, sitting under a banyan tree, holding a baby with AIDS."

Hey, why not?

But when did Rick Warren start sounding like Castro?

There is a religious Left in our country. (We love you, Catholic Worker.) Rick Warren isn't among them. But I like it when the religious Right starts actually talking about the things Jesus talked about—feeding the poor and healing the sick—and there's been precious little of it since Jerry Falwell and his Moral Majority took control of the airwaves and the agenda back in the eighties.

What did Jesus say about abortion and gays? Not a goddamn syllable. He did, however, have a few thoughts on Mammon.

That's why it was terribly interesting to see Kansas Senator Sam Brownback take to Warren's pulpit.

The little I knew of Brownback was from reading Thomas Frank's marvelous *What's the Matter With Kansas?* (Answer: a lot!) I knew Brownback had converted to Opus Dei-style Catholicism and made his bones on such issues as Third-World sex slavery and, of course, abortion. (He had originally gotten involved in Kansas politics, however, as a pro-choice moderate.) I also knew that in his original post as Kansas ag secretary—not elected or appointed by the governor, but actually chosen by the heads of the agriculture industry!— he had made limits on dangerous herbicides "voluntary," and he never found a thorny issue, either there or in the House, that couldn't be fixed with deregulation. Unless, of course, that issue took place on your queen-size bed.

So who would have ever, ever thought that Sam Brownback is charming and hilarious?

Boyish at fifty, he started out with love words for Obama—the topic for this session was "We Must Work Together"—and a story of having to precede him at a meeting of the NAACP. "They were very polite, and couldn't have been kinder, but when Barack followed, it was like, 'Oh, Elvis is here.' This time I'm more comfortable," he continued. "Welcome to *my* house." (Obama would later ding him for that, in what seemed to be the only deviation from his prepared remarks. "One thing I got to say, though, Sam: this is my house too. This is *God*'s house." Cue fucking *giant* applause.)

And Brownback recited the 100th Psalm, and got choked up saying it. And he talked about Uganda, and AIDS, and genocide. "If we will just give them the crumbs off our table," he said, and then repeated it, "they will live, and we will save our souls." He talked about Lazarus and the rich man, and said, "I think this is our country today." That's right: our country will burn because we turn our backs on those in need.

Wha???

The gaybashing hasn't been working so much lately, and abortion seems to have lost some of its electoral zing. Maybe that's why leaders in the evangelical movement are in the middle of a battle for the soul of their church. Joel C. Hunter resigned as head of the Christian Coalition two weeks ago before he had even taken the post; he had wanted the Coalition to focus on poverty and global warming (the evangelicals call this—and I got no problem with it— "creation care"). Ted Haggard, before the Recent Unpleasantness with the gay masseuse and methamphetamines, had as head of the National Association of Evangelicals focused on the same. Maybe that's why Focus on the Family's James Dobson doesn't have time to cure him of The Gay.

Even Sam Brownback is talking the talk, and that's all to the good.

As for Obama, well, it was good to see him, and it was great to hear someone say the word *condoms* from the Saddleback pulpit. ("Fidelity is the ideal," he said, "but we are dealing with flesh-and-blood men and women, not abstractions." His call for condoms instead of expecting abstinence didn't draw huge applause, but it drew enough to impress me.)

But let's take another lesson from the Book: when Rick Warren and Sam Brownback, my prodigal sons, return to me and talk of poverty and AIDS (and separation of church and state!) I throw them a party despite all the rest of them.

But when my dutiful son Obama says, "It has been too easy for some to point to the unfaithful husband, or the promiscuous youth *or the gay man* and say, 'This is your fault. You have sinned.' [But] my faith reminds me that we are all sinners" (my emphasis), well, I don't seem to give him credit for his miles more of good than Brownback and Warren. Instead I just kind of want to smack him in the mouth for even letting that kind of statement stand. There's just no pleasing some people (me). Fuck you, Obama.

Call me!

How Green Was My Valley

I was a little leery of driving into the blizzard: I've driven off a cliff. I've been smashed in the face with a rock that took out my eye. I've bled internally, my brave little ovaries on a suicide mission against their occupying cysts. It would be just like me to get trapped in a deadly Tsunami of Snow! But my friend is a real man and, as such, has a Jeep with real-man tires. We would be *fine*.

And since it was New Year's and I've got a long-standing tradition (like all my other traditions, a terribly fine one) of waking someplace beautiful to watch the sun rise on the new year, it was necessary that we drive into the mountains. In the blizzard. And like Mary and Joseph or something, without any reservations at the inn.

But Jesus loves us, as you already knew, and after we drove into Wrightwood, where Honda CRXs were attempting to drive the icy highway in the blizzard sans chains, and where there was no room, and after we went into Crestline, where there was no snow and they not only wouldn't let us smoke in the rooms, but they also wouldn't let us smoke outside them, and after we went to Running Springs, which was like the goddamn city, all dirty snow and traffic-jammed, where a man stopped his car to let his wife out at the grocery store, and she stood and changed her shoes with the car door open as people waited to turn behind them, completely unaware she was blocking traffic *on a highway* (I don't think she was overly entitled so much as totally clueless that other people exist in the world; had she known—had my friend allowed me to explain it to her, gently and politely—I'm sure she would have been very apologetic indeed), well, then we said, "Let's try this here Green Valley Lake." And we did, four miles out a stupidly beautiful, icy road, through virgin snow and past leafless trees whose every branch and twig were frozen, the sun shining gold through icicles blown up by the wind until they looked like birds in flight.

And there had been a cancellation, and we could have the very last cabin for a price that wasn't too terribly dear, and people waved from their yards (there was a snowman in every yard and a chicken in every pot), and our little lane had snow piled on both sides of its steep little self (till it seemed we were on the Canadian luge team every time we drove it), and our cabin was the dearest thing you've ever seen, homey and kind and embanked in the snow, and the owners had left some black truffle oil from Trader Joe's, with which we marinated our New York steaks, and we were very well-pleased indeed.

So as everyone is bitching that Jan Egeland of the UN dared to call America "stingy" vis-à-vis our tsunami relief—and actually, outraged and bombastic AM radio personages, he *didn't*; he said rich Western nations were stingy when it came to relief for Third-World nations in general, and we *are*—well, let us know that we are pure in our hearts. After all, I gave Doctors Without Borders a hundred clams this week—or precisely one-fourth of what I spent on my fabulous New Year's getaway two days later. So that's good, right? Isn't it?

In our little lakeside town, where we witnessed a man stop his SUV to pluck a stray piece of garbage from a slush puddle, there was a little pizza place. It would have music and dancing for New Year's Eve, a sign informed us, and so we went. But the band didn't make it up the mountain ("They're from Long Beach," the manager told us, but he couldn't remember their names; still, they must be flakey Long Beach friends of ours, but when we called a few, none of them copped to it), and so the evening's entertainment was a tinny boom box playing Willie Nelson. It was fine by us, as well as the other five customers, until a bunch of OC kids in Angels caps trooped in at 11:15 p.m. It was, in a word, delightful.

The next day, after we sledded and tobogganed and played and cavorted, we went back to our little Kinkadian cabin (so Kinkadian it should have had a trademark symbol and the title *Hearthlight*), stuffed ourselves again and watched movies all night long.

And it was while I was watching *Dirty Dancing*—"But it's *sexy!*" I told my friend, who wouldn't watch; "They're *sexy* at each other!"—that I began to wonder if it wasn't, as he had claimed, the bad writing, bad acting and bad eighties music when they're supposed to be in the sixties, etc., that were bothering him, but the main plot twist: an illegal abortion.

I never asked him, so I don't know.

I'm a pro-life Democrat, so it's doubtful they'd let me chair the Democratic National Committee. And Commie Mom and I and all other progressive, pro-life Dems have always been sneered at by our pro-choice friends. They're really appalled with us, that we would sentence their daughters to die in back alleys. And so we've downplayed it; we don't say it that often; and even in my heart, abortion has faded until it just isn't that big a deal. My priorities are with the poor who are already born, and if they play their cards right or Jimmy Carter comes calling, I might even give them another hundred bones.

The Right are ridiculous: no abortions, but no sex ed. No birth control. No prenatal care. No welfare to help out those poor women who carried their babies to term. And when someone's mama's neglected him while she got kicked off welfare and worked two jobs, and a six-year-old takes his uncle's gun to school and kills a girl, well, call for the death penalty for the little monster.

The Left's better, but not by much: Was that really NOW lobbying against Connor's Law (for Lacy Peterson's unborn son), which would make it a crime to kill a fetus in an attack on the mother? Now you're just being an asshole.

So what's my answer? I gave it a lot of thought after I watched *Dirty Dancing*—it's a thought-provoking movie, that one, especially when Patrick Swayze kisses Jennifer Grey's neck just so—and you're not going to like my solution. Nobody is. *Everybody* will be unhappy, which is how I know it's the right answer for all.

The Answer: outlaw abortion—if you're over twenty years of age. If you're twenty-two and can't figure out how to use the Pill, you can damn well live with it and carry the baby to term and give it up for adoption in a humane manner. It's not the fifties; unless you're a Virginia schoolteacher, you still get to keep your job.

But for teenage girls, there should be abortion on demand—no waiting period, no parental notification, not even a co-pay. Teenage girls are the ones who will actually kill themselves if they think their parents might find out—

and their parents just might beat them to death if they do. Teenage girls are the only segment of society who could be actually endangered by unwanted pregnancies, and they should get a do-over. Sin? In my Church, yes. But better than Daddy sending you to your Maker with the Word of the Lord.

easter vacation

Last Friday—Good Friday—my small buttercup of a son asked me how Jesus died.

My small buttercup of a son is 10 years old. And so it occurs to me I may have neglected his religious education.

I wonder if it makes it better or worse that Thursday—Holy Thursday, the night of the Last Supper (which perhaps I'll mention to him, now that I think of it)—my small buttercup of a son met Marilyn Manson.

"Hi," Manson said to my boy. "I'm Manson."

"Hi," my boy said in his soft little voice. And then Andy Dick came up and started hitting my boy in the head, so I smacked his glasses off his face. Cue the Crystals: and then he kissed me.

I put my hand on Andy Dick's face and pushed him away. "I'm really fucked-up," he told me perkily. "I'm looking for cocaine!"

"Let me know how that works out for you!" I told him, and then I puked.

I didn't actually puke right then: it was later, on our way home, when I told my gay to pull over, got out of the car and puked on someone's tree. Frankly, the tree had seen better days.

"That was four drinks on no dinner," I told my gay the next morning when he called to laugh at me. "Now imagine *eight*."

Eight was the magic number of shots of gin Jane Doe had been given, in addition to pot to smoke and beer to chug, the night the Haidl Gang had their playful way with her inert body. And the night before, on the way up to our fabulous Hollywood party where my boy met Marilyn Manson and I slapped the glasses off Andy Dick's face, my gay had said, "I don't understand why Greg Haidl and the other kids are gonna get serious jail time if they were all just playing around sexually."

"You didn't read any of our coverage, did you?" I accused. "You only read the *Times* and *Register!*"

I told him about the defense neurologist I'd seen on the stand who kept inserting his talking point—that the sixteen-year-old Jane Doe was conscious and so "knew" she was "with three males." He kept repeating it: "She knows she is with three males."

"She is fully capable of exercising reasonable judgment," he said when looking at a sliver of videotape that apparently showed her moving hair from her face. "She is aware that she is with three males."

Before that, while watching a portion of tape in which Doe is drinking a beer—clearly *before* she passed out, as she is drinking a beer—the same neurologist kept repeating, "While she's drinking a beer, she is not comatose and not stuporous."

Wow.

And then I told my gay about the day the jury came in with its mostly guilty verdicts. (They acquitted Haidl, son of a multimillionaire assistant sheriff, on assault with a deadly weapon—the famous pool cue—and hung on rape by intoxication; Haidl's posse, Keith Spann and Kyle Nachreiner, racked up a few more acquittals and hung juries on their respective thirds of the 27 counts.)

I told him about Nachreiner, who'd spent most of the trial mad-dogging media and witnesses, crouching in the doorway to the restroom and sobbing before we ever went into the courtroom. I told him about Spann pushing into the courtroom a friend in a wheelchair; I'd thought it was to garner sympathy and didn't know that the friend, who looked like a teenage boy, was Spann's grief-stricken—and cancer-stricken—mother. I told him about how loud the cuffs were as the deputies snapped them on the boys' wrists after the verdicts, how they echoed for a long minute throughout the silent (except for the sobbing) room. I told him about the jury foreman, a 27-year-old guy with tats, a goatee, cut-off skate shorts and sunglasses on the back of his bald head, and how the one time I'd attended the trial before the verdicts, I'd heard him talking to other jurors about music, how all the bands he cited were intelligent, indie bands, and how I knew then that if the defense thought he was some kind of piggy, misogynist thug because he had tats, they were going to be very surprised.

I told my gay that, yes, she was a tramp, and so were all of us at some point or other (at least any of us who are interesting), but that didn't mean the boys got to knock her out and insert a pool cue, a Snapple bottle, a juice can, and a lit cigarette into her vagina while she was unconscious. I told him about Dana Parsons' latest column in the *LA Times*, in which he said boys should take note of the handcuffs on the Haidl thugs but also warned, "To girls who think it's cool or necessary to engage in promiscuous sex, think of Jane Doe."

"Yeah," my gay said sheepishly. "I only read the coverage in the *Times* and *Register*."

Not only did my son not know how Jesus died, and not only did I puke in front of him, and not only did I let Andy Dick get within twenty yards of him, but it was also a school night. It was not my finest mothering hour.

But the party was an art opening for the luscious seventies photographic portraits of Mick Rock. The people were gorgeous and cultured and very polite (with the exception, as always, of Andy Dick). My boy has always been immersed in music and politics and the world's best goings-on. And like my parents before me, I've always erred on the side of telling my boy the truth about things and preparing him for adulthood. My boy, for the entirety of the Haidl conversation, had on his *Old School* earmuffs, but he does know what rape is, so he can know when he's older that he's *not to do it.*

And when he asks about Jesus, I tell him what Jesus said about the poor and how we are to treat our neighbors and that Jesus was the greatest prophet who ever lived, but maybe didn't come back to life three days after the Romans crucified him, but that a lot of people believe he did. For Easter, we didn't go to Mass; we had a beautiful picnic at Commie Mom's beach.

And I tell him no, he may not go to youth group with our really, really nice neighbor boys who are really, really nice, but their not believing in evolution is *not acceptable*, and I won't have him coming home from youth group believing Mommy's going to hell.

Hell comes after eight shots of Bombay.

SECTION THREE

Sex, Drugs And Rock
& Roll, But Mostly Sex

The Domestic Life of a Porn Star

Porn stars are different from you and me. They have more sex

Candy Apples and her new husband, Bill Nance, live the Huntington Beach dream: pit bulls and a housegirl to watch them. But will the newly busty blonde with the sweet blue eyes ever stop taking it up the ass to pay for it all? A day in the life . . .

Do you remember that scene in *Boogie Nights* in which Marky Mark and his buddies go to rob the crazy coked-out guy with the lush eighties pad, his silk robe open, the powder flowing, the drugged-out Chinese houseboy wandering around throwing firecrackers, the state-of-the-art stereo booming out "Night Ranger" at about a million decibels? Porn star Candy Apples' life is nothing like that—except for the houseboy, who in this case is a plump, pretty, wholesome-looking nineteen-year-old redhead named Natalie.

Natalie has been sleeping on the couch for about two months. Her job is to watch the two pit bulls, Nigel and Cleopatra, whenever Candy and Bill want to leave the one-bedroom Huntington Beach apartment, even for a little while.

The apartment is plain. It has a barren little patio, a smallish kitchen, and a leopard-print rug over gray beach carpet to mark the sitting area. The bathroom is spotless, decorated by a couple of pretty blue candles. The only other decorations in the house—besides the Pokémon motif, from the Japanese kid's cartoon to which all three say they're addicted—are the cow skull over the giant TV and a framed Tom Byron photo, inscribed, "To Candy: I wanna ram my big cock up your shithole and then make you suck it, you whore!!!" Five bent-over women, displaying their assholes and snatches like collies in heat, complete the composition. There is a desk and an ugly file cabinet with neat red folders holding her pictures, which look fantastic. Someone has arranged the video games very tidily on the entertainment center.

That compulsively clean someone was probably Candy herself—the woman *Hustler*'s Dick Pursel describes as "the very top of the very bottom of the barrel. She can act, and she's likable, and she seems a bit smarter than most. But she'll do anything." It seems even porn stars are subject to your mother's warnings: men only want good girls. If only they knew how very domestic she is.

Bill and Candy are friendly and fearless; Natalie is a little more shy, though she warms up later, when the subject is boys. But of the three, only Bill doesn't seem to recognize that there are maybe things you don't say to a person with a notepad. We are having lunch at a Mexican restaurant around the corner. Bill has ordered the no. 5 for Candy and is telling me about her insomnia. "She has to take sleeping pills!" he exclaims so I'll understand the depth of the problem. They exchange a look. "Just Excedrin PM," Candy clarifies—fast. She's a lot more comfortable joking about the twenty tokes it'll take her to get to sleep. Though both are faultlessly polite and friendly with me, they never look directly at the waiter or thank the busboy, who refills our waters several times.

Candy and Bill are both twenty-six, though he looks younger, despite his goatee and tattoos of blond bondage babes (from the cover of *Devil in Miss Jones 6*) running down his arms. He's a little bit roly-poly, too. He does not look threatening in the slightest, even though he wears the HB bad-boy uniform. She looks a little older than twenty-six, though not by much— twenty-nine perhaps. It's because she's so very thin. She's pretty, though not stunning. Her blue eyes are huge, and her roots are only a couple of shades ashier than her long blond hair. She has a small chin and a couple of patches of adult acne that are very skillfully covered in her sizzling promo pictures and video box covers. She is thinking about having her eyebrows tattooed on so she'll never have to draw them again. She says she's done almost 400 films.

She dresses down during the day in jeans that bag around her tiny ass, maroon Etnies from which she has removed the jingle bell that Natalie fastened—with a warning not to do it again—and a white tank top upon which is emblazoned, "I love porn." She doesn't need a bra, although her breasts seem enormous on her ribby frame. But though they look huge, they're in fact a very reasonable 480 ccs of saline. During the day, when we flit from one tattoo shop to the next, the talk will center on many women's recent boob jobs, and numbers like 600, 650 and 700 will be tossed around. "The other night, she was looking at 'em," Bill says, "and she goes, 'God, they look small! I want 'em bigger!'" It's shop talk. Everyone knows where everyone else got her boobs done. Almost everyone around here goes to a Dr Nicolli. Also, there's a guy who does boobs in Tijuana, though he's certified here. That way, he doesn't have to use such an expensive anesthesiologist. Candy and Bill paid $4,550—no Tijuana for them—and are well-pleased with the result. Bill can tell you which doctor in Utah is good—they were going to go to him, but he couldn't see them in time to do her boobs before the gang bang—and which doctor isn't. "A whole lotta people got bad jobs from the one guy," Bill tells me.

The gang bang? Candy is the new record holder, taking the title from Houston in October, with 742 men penetrating her in one way or another. Last I had heard, Annabelle Chong had the record, but apparently there've been five or six new world champions since. "I wasn't even sore!" Candy exclaims, her voice low and loud. "They stick it in, it counts. Head counts. Guys literally came up, put it in for two seconds, and got pulled off for the next guy. Normally, they would have had a little more time, but because the fire marshal was there . . ."

Bill breaks in. He always talks in exclamations. "The guy got the wrong permits! We were supposed to get married at the gang bang, but because the cops broke it up, we couldn't! There were, like, thirty cop cars! She ran into the makeup room and put her clothes on, and two huge bodyguards ran her down the stairs and into the limo!"

Candy and Bill got married in her parents' backyard instead, with a simple Hawaiian theme. Bill's grandparents and most of his aunts and uncles boycotted the wedding. They knew what she did, she says, and loved her anyway, until friends and neighbors saw her on *Howard Stern*. "Howard was wonderful to me," Candy says wistfully. "He was so nice! I didn't have to get naked; he didn't ask to see my boobs or anything!"

The publicity they could not forgive. But crowned in orchids, she looked lovely.

Together a little more than a year, though they've known each other for ten, the two are homebodies. Candy says she likes being domestic, and I believe her. Later, she will dawdle for an hour in the bathroom getting ready to go out, but when she's done, everything will have been returned to its proper place. You wouldn't even know she'd been in there. She likes to cook, she says. Bill and Natalie both exclaim what a good cook she is. What in her repertoire does Bill like best? He thinks about it for a second before his eyes light up, and he says, "She makes really good nachos!"

"Everything she makes is good," contends Natalie.

They smoke tons of dope, but they only party three or four times a year— "at the most!" says Bill. "That's the reason we moved from LA back to Huntington! The tweaking! You get caught up in that whole LA party scene. Every night, someone has an orgy. Girls on sets will lock themselves in the bathroom and smoke crack."

"I have a friend who couldn't work anywhere that wasn't in the vicinity of a methadone clinic," Candy says. "These girls have stick bodies, no butts and huge fake boobs. It's not healthy." But Candy and Bill will tell a tattoo artist friend later that day that they're thinking of moving back to the Valley. "You can get a five-bedroom house, with a pool and Jacuzzi, on an acre of land, for $1,200 per month," Bill will say. He will not mention the party scene.

Some porn stars, oddly, live in the beige suburbs of Irvine and Mission Viejo. But most stick to Huntington Beach: out of only about three hundred to five hundred people working in porn at any one time, Shelby and Pat Myne, Regan Starr, Dayton Rains, and Billy Glide, among others, live here. But Dayton has been off the radar for a while.

"People just disappear," Bill says. "She flaked on our bachelor party, flaked on our wedding, and we haven't heard from her since. Her number's disconnected . . ."

"We used to talk to her every day," Candy says sadly.

Nonetheless, Huntington Beach is the perfect antidote to the outside world's condemnation. A caller to a radio program may scream at her, "You're a whore! You're a whore!" But around here, she's well-insulated. Porn stars are at the top of the local entertainment heap, and Candy can deflect the screaming with a well-defended speech about "personal preference."

Go ahead. Tell her that most women feel porn stars give men license to look at all women as just three-holed fuckdolls. Candy will deftly announce, "I'm almost always the aggressor! How can that be demeaning or degrading to women?"

And around Huntington Beach, people buy it. Porn stars are sought after to give clubs more juice—Club Rubber alone sometimes feels as if it has more porn stars than paying customers, and in fact that's where Bill and Candy had their joint bachelor party. Lowest-denominator thrash-rock bands flaunt porn stars and strippers as arm candy. Daimon's sushi bar, in nearby Sunset Beach, is known and loved for its porn star clientele. Just try getting up to the sushi bar on a Thursday, Friday or Saturday night. You can't swing a raw fish without smacking a plastic breast.

Back at their apartment, the neighbor kid is hanging out front with Natalie. He is drinking a tall Bud from a paper bag. "Nobody's really at work around here," Candy explains. "Everyone's home."

"Where we live," Bill says, "you're either a stripper or a drug dealer or you own a clothing company."

"I know a lot of girls who are eighteen, and their dream is to become a stripper," Candy says. "[Costa Mesa-based clothing company] Black Flys are gods down here; they made the whole scene in this area. Everyone's a snow-boarder or a skater, and they get everything for free, and that's all they need." She continues with a point I have never heard raised, and I'm surprised: "Plus, I think it's hard around here to get a real job."

The scene is incredibly *Peter Pan* or, for those of you who saw it, *Marie Baie des Anges*. In that film, two very bad and very beautiful children fall in love in the woodsy paradise of the French Mediterranean. No parents are ever in evidence. In Candy's case, though, parents are in evidence: Candy's parents, both retired, and married—to each other!—for thirty-five years, talk to her almost daily.

She was living at home when she started making movies at nineteen. Her parents knew she worked for a porn production company, but once they realized she was also starring, they made her move out. "I didn't talk to them for, like, a year," Candy says. "But now they realize I'm stable and paying my own bills and stuff."

I ask how much she makes. She says she gets up to $2,000 per scene and works ten to twenty days per month. But if she's making, say, $200,000 per year, I don't see any evidence of it in their modest apartment.

"The first four years, she probably made a million dollars," says Bill. "But you spend it as fast as you make it. If you make $1,000, you'll spend it because you're thinking, 'I can make another thousand tomorrow.' Clothes. Partying."

"I'd have five guys living with me," Candy says, "and I wouldn't necessarily be sleeping with them, but I'd be home so I'd want them to be home, for company."

"So she's getting six people's bills . . . ," Bill says.

Now she gets three people's bills. She's restoring their credit, she says. And saving for the future? "Yes," Candy says shortly.

Around 1 p.m. on a Friday, bowls are smoked. Candy, after much puttering, finally finds the earrings she took out of her nipples; she wants to stretch her earlobes with them. Then it's off to Newport Tattoo on the Balboa Peninsula. Next door to the tattoo parlor, people are hanging around outside a bar, smoking. A truck is parked out front; two boxers sit quietly inside, waiting for their master. After the piercer, a friend of theirs whom they haven't seen for a while, stretches Candy's ears and puts new balls on Bill's earrings, Bill hands him a $20. He always carries the money, although Candy is the one who makes it, and I think to myself that she's smart. She'll never let him feel like less of a man. *He* is lover, chauffeur and watcher in one. *She* pays the bills and likes anal. In the year they've been together, they've spent three days apart: when Keith Richards, "who is a really big fan," flew her to Vegas for a Stones video shoot. How often do Candy and Bill have sex? Every day. "I pout if I don't get it every day," Bill says, laughing. "He wakes me up at 5:30 in the morning," Candy grumbles good-naturedly. But she loves him, and aside from her job and those 742 men, she sleeps only with him.

At 4 p.m., Bill and Candy go to their friend Jimmy's house. He is adding flowers and vines to the "Porn Star" tattooed on her lower back. She winces the whole time. "This one fucking kills," she says. She has a fairy on her neck and tattoos above both breasts. But the lower back hurts like hell. By about 7:30, Jimmy is done. From then on, Candy will greet everyone they see with, "My back hurts sooo bad!" She is excited about her tattoo, and they will spend twenty minutes at a time discussing it before a few moments of silence. Then they will discuss it some more.

We go over to Candy's friend Pilar's to pick up the pants she borrowed, and Candy insists that I sit in front. She swears she likes the back seat, and I don't know if she's just being polite to a guest or if she maybe likes the feeling that she's being chauffeured. Then it's back to the apartment again. Bill's little sister is there, hanging out with her best friend: Natalie.

While Candy gets ready to go out, we watch *Greed*. One team answers that "com" in "dot-com" stands for "communications." No $100,000 for you! Bill talks about his tattoo (some more, actually; this has been going on a while) and then recounts to Natalie and his sister tonight's *Blind Date* episode, which included a chick getting finger-banged in a taxicab. We all discuss the merits of the show, which wanted to pay Candy $400 to appear. "Why would I want to do that?" she asks. "I'm married."

Candy appears in the living room with two tops: one is a maroon push-up number, which she's currently modeling, and the other is a fuzzy, lime-green teeny tube top. "What do you think, babe?" she asks her husband. We all agree that the green will look marvelous in the black light at the Tap House. She puts it on, and I realize the maroon number wasn't pushing her up at all. Her breasts were doing that all by themselves.

The three of us head to the Tap House; we are on the list, thanks to Bill and Candy. Once inside, I spot Bear, a bouncer I know from Club 369, and am quickly passed six drink tickets. It's the most natural thing in the world to immediately hand the tickets to Bill to hold. I seem to be channeling Candy: the man should be in charge of the drinks.

Candy dances a bit but mostly stands next to her husband while he chats with their friends. When the rose girl appears, everyone pretends not to see her—it's the only way you can deal with a rose girl, really—except for Bill. He buys a pink rose for his sweetheart and a white one for me. They both really are very thoughtful. Outside, we see local promoter extraordinaire Altan. This is who Candy meant when she said she was engaged as a teen to a man she'd been with for five years. But he cheated on her, she said, so she started sleeping with all his friends. Then she got into the business. She really likes having sex with midgets. "I just think they're so cute," she says.

After a while, I head home, two of Candy's films on the seat beside me. In one, Candy looks gorgeous, thick black-framed glasses giving her the librarian look. In the other, *Trixxx*—a pretty high-budget takeoff of Keanu Reeves' *Matrix*—she accommodates two giant, condomless cocks at once, one in her ass and the other in her pussy, which is shaved like a child's. One man chokes her until her face turns red. Although she has told me flatly that she doesn't come at work—only with her Bill—she groans as though she's being slaughtered, then gets on her knees and frenetically moves her mouth from one man to the other. She looks like a madwoman. When she spits out their come, her eyes rolling back in her head, it looks as though she's rabid. She is not worried about AIDS in the slightest, she says. Everyone gets tested once a month. I turn it off.

And what about Natalie? She's going to get a tattoo with her baby daughter's name. She has no plans for the future. Bill and Candy give her pocket money for cigarettes, though surprisingly neither of them smokes. Bill and Candy don't like her boyfriend. One morning, they tell me, she was throwing up because she'd gotten really drunk and didn't usually drink at all. On the phone, her boyfriend asked her if she was pregnant. "Maybe," she answered, to which he responded, "I don't think we should see each other anymore." And hung up. "He gets mad at her if she doesn't answer the phone fast enough," Candy says disbelievingly—and before we had gone to the Tap House, he called. Natalie's first words to him were, "I was outside, smoking!" A look passed between Candy and Bill. "She didn't answer the phone fast enough," Candy confirmed. In the same phone call, Natalie and her boyfriend argued about whether she could go see him or not. She tells us what transpired. "I told him, 'I even had an offer to babysit for fifteen bucks and a ride out there. But I have to stay here.' And he's saying I'm not making him a priority!" Bill and Candy do not take the hint to give her the night off from dog-watching.

Bill thinks Natalie should get into the business. "She's a free-love girl. I'm going, 'Dude! If you're gonna do that, you might as well get paid for it!'" Candy says Natalie is going to go on the set with her next week. "She says she wants to get into movies," Candy says noncommittally. Candy doesn't seem to be pushing her too hard, and I suspect that Natalie is just saying she wants to get into movies so Bill and Candy will be happy—like when she said, "Shit! We missed *Pokémon* today! And I even thought about it at 1:18. I looked at the clock, and thought, 'Oh, good! We still have 45 minutes!'" The whole thing sounds rehearsed, and I suspect she only likes *Pokémon* so she and Candy and Bill will have an additional bond. Natalie seems to have a major crush on the neighbor kid's friend, whom she breathlessly describes as "the really, really cute one." He's okay-looking, but when I point that out, she immediately agrees with me. "He's got a bad attitude about women," she says, changing from admirer to mild critic. "He lives in a rehab. He's almost thirty, like, twenty-seven or something!" Old.

Candy and Bill say everyone in porn—Candy excluded—has a story. Molested, abused, something. But Candy's parents were wonderful and very normal, they say. Should anyone be looking for a perfect porn queen, though, one with low enough self-esteem to think the alcoholic neighbor's friend is the epitome of manliness, Natalie might be the $64,000 answer.

george bush's joint

Marijuana can be addictive. Marijuana isn't great for learning or short-term memory. Marijuana's not the best thing for children—the best things for children are *fresh air, sunshine* and *love*! And if you own a bong (or "water pipe," as the head shops insist upon calling them), the chances are good that you smoke way too much dope. *Nobody* really needs a bong.

Can we all stipulate to that?

The White House's Office of National Drug Control Policy wants us to stipulate to a little more: that marijuana is far more dangerous than it was when the Boomers smoked it (the Boomers, of course, can't refute this by admitting to smoking it still); that marijuana will turn our precious tots into dropouts who rob banks; that marijuana is, in fact, a scourge upon our youth. To do this, they threw a party. Okay, it wasn't so much a party as a panel put on for the SoCal media, but I love panels, and the sandwiches were excellent.

Tuesday afternoon, I got an invite for the "Marijuana & Kids" media briefing in San Diego the next day. Fantastic. A few minutes later, my dad called to check in and have a nice gossip. My dad is a recovering addict (mostly coke and other uppers) who owns and runs a treatment center in Malibu and also publishes the online magazine *Heroin Times*. It's a non-judgmental look at all the facets of heroin addiction, providing information on how to kick it, obits from grieving parents, editorials on the Drug War and referrals on where to get clean.

Would my dad come with me to San Diego? We could board the Amtrak right in Santa Ana and have a delightful day together under the auspices of the White House Office of National Drug Control Policy. It would be the best day ever!

My dad said yes!

The whole way down to San Diego, we drank coffee in the Coastliner's lounge car and watched the folks on their way to the Del Mar racetrack troop boisterously in for more rounds of beers and Bloody Marys. It was 10:30 a.m. A young blond guy several beers in sat with headphones on and stared at me. We avoided his reddened gaze and chatted instead with a man who had overheard us guffawing about the conference to which we were headed.

I'm not a member of the National Organization for the Repeal of Marijuana Laws (those NORML cats can party!), but I think prohibitions against pot are preposterous. I find especially outrageous the $170 million budget of the Office of National Drug Control Policy—and that's just for ad campaigns and media buys. It doesn't count the billions spent on black helicopters and Agent Orange for spraying on farms in South America. I even thought Johnny Depp's recent quote about buying pot for his kids when they get older was the most responsible bit of parenting I'd heard in some time.

I grew up with a daddy who was a drug addict, and I have a pretty good grasp on "harmful." Harmful and I go way back. And the occasional pot smoker ain't it.

Take two drinks at dinner? Get giggly at a party? You're probably okay. Get smashed on rye and drive with your kid in the car? You're probably not. And it viscerally pisses me off when people try to conflate the two. The Office of National Drug Control Policy wants us to know it's a "myth" that marijuana is "harmless." Thanks for the straw man, Office of National Drug Control Policy. Nobody said it was, but for the vast majority of otherwise law-abiding citizens who smoke dope once in a while, it's fine. In fact, we even have a young family member who *is* addicted to pot; we've had loads of fabulous interventions for him that didn't take, but now that he's a little bit older, he seems to be letting go of all his dropout, no-job lameness all by himself. Right now he's in school *and* has a part-time job, and we're very encouraged. Addiction to pot is bad, but even so, he has yet to violently rob a bank. The only person he's hurting is his long-suffering mother, who has to scrimp to pay his rent. Being lazy isn't against the law—yet.

So don't get addicted; keep it to the equivalent of a drink at dinner, and it'll probably lower your blood pressure and cure your glaucoma. I'd like to see the "liberal" mainstream media admit that just once.

Going to the media briefing on "Marijuana & Kids" from the Office of National Drug Control Policy, I had, you could say, an agenda.

The guy on the train lives in a Laguna Beach halfway house and was on his way to Tijuana to gamble. His sponsors say he has given up one addiction for another, but he never bets more than he can afford to lose. He never bets his rent. You know what I say? That that's probably fine.

With the ocean to the west, my dad fielded phone calls from his staff about this or that client melting down into pockmarked piles of sobbing flesh (and one who was having a herpes outbreak and needed an Acyclovir scrip—stat!). Drugs are bad, and herpes is too, but not one of his clients is in there for marijuana dependency; they're in for really icky stuff, like junk and crack. Stuff that will kill you or cause you to leave your baby in the crib for three days while you go on a mission, unlike pot. An hour later, the Office of National Drug Control Policy would try to tell us otherwise. Its panel of San Diego experts repeatedly conflated numbers of people court-ordered into rehab with numbers of people addicted to marijuana, for instance, even though if you're caught with pot, you're ordered into rehab regardless of whether or not you're an addict.

Yes, the Office of National Drug Control Policy had lots of statistics. The only problem was their stats kept contradicting their other stats, but they kept repeating them just the same. It was kind of like a prosecutor who tries two supposed accomplices separately, changing the facts in each trial so he can argue that *this* was the perp who had pulled the trigger. Perfectly legal according to the appellate courts, but kind of stinky, don't you think?

We walked from the lovely train depot through a Caltrans war zone on Pacific Highway to the San Diego County Administration Building; engraved on the front of the grand, tall building was the legend "Good Government Demands the Intelligent Interest of Every Citizen." We had to enter from the side; the front doors are closed so terrorists can't come in. Works from a civic art exhibition lined the walls of the first floor—citizens' sweet watercolors of frogs and Mission architecture. On the third floor, two female aides were waiting to greet us and point us into the right room. They knew who we were because we had RSVP'd, but there was still a moment of paranoia on my part. I really wish I knew what was in my FBI file.

We sat in the second row of a conference room that was perhaps 7 percent full. A few local news stations sent cameras; they wouldn't have much to film, but we all got swell press packs, helpfully complemented with notepads and pens. Those of us who were *real* journalists already had our own long notebooks, and we wielded them proudly. There seemed to be three of us. (The other nine or ten attendees, it would turn out, were representing for marijuana task forces and local treatment centers. The task forcers would go on to spout really wild-eyed statements during the question segment. Fun!) We looked through press packets brimming with stat sheets and releases. On the very first page, the fourth bullet point stated, "In [fiscal year] 2001, 42.2 percent of federally sentenced offenders in Southern California had committed a drug offense. Of that total, 76.8 percent involved marijuana."

Good god: more than three-fourths of all drug offenders were sentenced for pot? Pot? Isn't that statistic usually trumpeted by people who are *against* the drug war? Are communist moles in the Office of National Drug Control Policy trying to undermine its mission? Most citizens would think that's a big waste of jail space, especially since "more than 83 million Americans (37 percent) ages 12 and older have tried marijuana at least once." That comes from the Office of National Drug Control Policy's press packet too, and that would be a *lot* of new jail cells!

A short time after we sat down, the National Youth Anti-Drug Media Campaign's deputy director, Robert Denniston—he introduced himself as "Bob"—called us to order and introduced the panel. First was Thomas Alexander, a shiny-headed black man in a beautiful black suit, from the county probation department. He had a gray mustache and a gentle demeanor. He would eventually advocate drug testing all teens before they entered high school.

Next was Igor Koutsenok, a psychiatrist and associate director of UC San Diego's Addiction Training Center. He told shocking truths that were immediately twisted back into drug-warriorese by the panel and the moderator. He had a richly rolling accent from east of the Elbe.

Linda Bridgeman Smith is the planning manager of San Diego County's Health and Human Services Agency's alcohol and drug services. She had soft brown eyes and rarely got to say anything.

Elizabeth Urquhart, director of adolescent services at the San Diego Phoenix House, had pretty, long blond hair. She was flashy and spouted nonsense that Igor (he told us, "Call me Igor!") had refuted only minutes before. She also gave warm, extremely condescending looks to the teen panelist . . .

Juan. A soft-spoken, eighteen-year-old man in a shirt and tie, Juan had shortly cropped hair and a goatee. I had remembered the invitation to the panel as touting the inclusion of an "actual teen!" but this turned out to be unfair on my part. The invitation merely stated "a teen who has experienced problems with marijuana will also join the conversation." My bad.

For forty-five minutes or so, we listened as Denniston posed questions to the panel. Denniston, a bespectacled, bearded man who looks like a shrink or a college professor, is an *excellent* face for the Office of National Drug Control Policy. He was *reasonable*, tossing objections out to the panel before the audience could. When Urquhart noted the number of "addicts" in treatment at Phoenix House, for instance, he asked how many of those had been court-ordered vs how many were self-identified. And he began reasonably as well, saying, "This is not about medical marijuana or legalization. Those are valid topics for debate, but they're not why we're here."

Valid topics for debate? Shut yo mouth!

When he introduced Juan, he noted that Juan had been clean and sober for more than a year. "That's great," he said gently. "We're very proud of you." And we were!

And when the probation department's Alexander kept mentioning how many of the young people he oversaw had "drug issues" (which I interpreted, correctly or incorrectly, as kids who had been caught with drugs, solely or in addition to their other crimes), Denniston smoothly prompted, "So those are young people with drug *problems*, correct?" Oh, yes, indeed, agreed Alexander. From then on, Alexander cited the number of youths under his supervision with "drug problems."

Denniston was very, very good. And did I mention he was reasonable?

When Juan (actual teen!) told us of his experiences and subsequent sobriety, Denniston told him kindly, "You were fortunate in a couple of ways. There was treatment available, for one." This is the kind of thing Californians especially, with our terribly sane policy of mandating treatment over jail when available, like to hear. Then he asked a really useful question, too: "What's the availability of treatment here in San Diego?" That is a superuseful question! Bridgeman Smith raised her hand, but Urquhart answered instead—before throwing another condescending simper at Juan.

Juan, by the way, started smoking pot at twelve or thirteen at the house of a friend who had a bad dealer brother. He also got hooked on meth and heroin, and when he OD'd (though probably not on pot), he decided he needed help. I think that was a fine decision.

Alexander agreed, adding, "Marijuana and meth are *very* interrelated."

Igor, the UCSD psychiatrist, gave us the 411 on how marijuana affects the brain. As we'd all suspected, it damages it. Luckily, "We've found the effects are reversible, so it's less severe than we thought." That's the good news. Later, when asked by one of the three journalists about the difference between how marijuana damages the brain and how good, old-fashioned bourbon damages the brain, he forthrightly stated, "Alcohol is much more toxic. From a chemical composition standpoint, it's worse. Much worse." Little bit off-message, Igor. And as John Ashcroft already knows, you really shouldn't let those pesky journalists in to media briefings at all.

Now Igor, remember, is *against* pot. But, to make sure we all got the point, Igor added, "There's no evidence marijuana by itself can trigger violent or criminal behavior. Alcohol definitely can." Eight separate pages in our handy press packets cited marijuana's links to violent and/or criminal behavior. Several had very large graphs, including the one titled, in 26-point type, "Marijuana Use Is Also Related to Other Delinquent Behaviors."

And twenty minutes later, the head of the local youth-marijuana task force stated from the audience, "For everyone who believes marijuana is 'Haight/Ashbury, go to the beach and listen to folk music,' I think the statistics will show that now it's 'toke up and go rob a liquor store.'"

Igor was getting off-message again. He had already explained that many of the people who become dependent on marijuana are using it to treat depression, when he explained to us, "We know that problems in school are not the *result* of substance abuse, but rather are a major factor in the *initiation* of substance abuse." (His emphasis.)

Do I really need to tell you how many pages in the press packet cited the relationship between pot and poor school performance?

Luckily, Denniston was there to set things right. "So you're saying, 'Let's not confuse cause and effect. Marijuana is not the cause of school failure, and school failure is not the cause of marijuana abuse, but it's *circular.*'"

Am I insane? Eh, probably so.

Then, during the panel's closing statements, the probation department's Alexander stated, "Parents ask me, 'What about testing? Should I test?' I say, have a plan. What are you gonna do if it's positive, and what are you gonna do if it's negative?"

Denniston: "That's an interesting conversation. It raises issues of trust and punishment versus treatment."

Alexander: "There's a carrot at the end of it, but you gotta test."

Since *I'm* not somebody who tries to win arguments by twisting things, I will be fair and point out that the parents he's telling that to are parents of kids who are already in the system.

Bridgeman Smith got to talk for a moment, saying the county is very supportive of treatment services. I'm very glad to hear that.

Urquhart talked about drug use and the behaviors that go along with it, including doing poorly in school. Was she not listening to Igor at all?

Juan said he had no closing statement. I like Juan. I'm glad he's clean.

After the panel discussion ended, Denniston came over to thank me for my questions (okay, I was the journalist who'd asked about pot and alcohol, plus a bunch of others that were too boring to go into on their "emergency room" statistics, which were just retarded, and some other stuff, too). I introduced my father and explained his magazine.

"Oh, so you probably advocate harm reduction?" Denniston asked.

"No, we don't advocate it, but we present all points of view without judgment," my dad rambled.

"We're not allowed to talk about harm reduction," Denniston chuckled. "Federal employee and all." Boy, he is so reasonable!

He's so reasonable he's probably even against Utah Republican Senator Orrin Hatch's "VICTORY" Act, which would expand the Patriot Act to include "narco-terrorism." Not that he'd ever say so, since he's a federal employee.

He's Mr Reasonable, in fact. Boy howdy, is Bob Denniston reasonable! He is not shrill at all, and we had a lovely chat about Cuba, among other things.

But when I called the next day to follow up on House Resolution 2086, the re-authorization of the Office on National Drug Control Policy, which includes the language, "take all steps necessary to oppose any attempt to legalize the use of a substance" (so tax dollars, for instance could be spent on partisan campaigns against a pro-legalization candidate), and to follow up on Denniston's role, if any, in the Super Bowl "smoking pot finances bin Laden" commercials and to ask some budget questions, why, my new pal Bob didn't call me back.

Nor the next day.

In fact, of all the panelists I called for follow-up (their numbers were very thoughtfully included in the press packets), only Igor ever answered his phone.

I've got eight pages, though, helpfully informing me of the relationship between marijuana use and delinquent behaviors.

smell the Love

Is the best thing about the Moseleys their clean close shave? No, it's waking up in their arms

The Moseleys are sex on a spit. They are greasy, fatty, love juice dripping onto sputtering flames. They will look into your eyes and quote romantic sayings from the John Hughes masterpiece *Sixteen Candles* and the current issue of *Cosmo*. They will look into your eyes and buy you a Scorpion—for lovers only— and then they will buy you another. They will look into your eyes and tell you one of them has an itch: the rock & roll itch. They attribute it to the weather: it's been so hot and moist lately.

The Moseleys work in their uncle's emery-board factory, which sets them to making all manner of lewd double-entendres about buffing. They are from Bakersfield and love raisins, for which they probably also have all manner of lewd double-entendres. They are a many-entendred beast. They have girl hair like Jon Bon Jovi and Richie Sambora, except Bon Jovi's hair, and Sambora's, is expensive and arguably attractive, while the Moseleys' looks like your grandma's circa 1960. They are losers. Man, are they losers. How loser-y are they? A lot! Yet every time I see them, my heart flaps around in my chest like a frightened bat.

This is not so much a story about the Moseleys—though it's that, too—as it is a story about why girls want them, them and all the fire-breathing rock stars like them who are bad and wrong in every way. Even the term "rock star," in the world of those of us who would love them, manages to be both an epithet and a longing sigh. Gwen Stefani says it . . . well, if not best, then at least most kittenishly: Why do the good girls always want the bad boys? It's a sad story— and a cautionary one. Be warned.

I have managed to miss the Moseleys' shows several times; I unerringly arrive just as they are packing their gear. Finally, on Earth Day, in the parking lot of the Hub in Fullerton, they are there, onstage.

There is Bunny Moseley, wielding his guitar like a three-foot penis and entreating us all to "drink the chalice." There is Grady, with dimples chiseled into his cheeks, railing (in a Kathleen Turner-cum-Madonna semi-British accent) against the Man forcing us to use his internal combustion engine and yowling instead for an engine powered by *rock & roll!* Just add three quarts of the Truth!

All right! All right!

Shadoobie!

And there is Rex—shy, quiet Rex—the bona fide Paul McCartney of the band, back when McCartney was really, really cute and hadn't yet become so unbelievably bougie and pretentious. Rex refuses to take off his wedding band, causing a major loss of sexy points since nice girls refuse to like married men, and Grady and Bunny harangue him about it to no effect. There is also a drummer of some kind—Palmsley, I believe?—his bob held back in cute lil barrettes. And then there is Harvey, on maracas. Harvey is squirrelly, like a retarded puppy. I am not in love with Harvey.

At the beginning of their set, I have a terrible cold and cannot breathe through my nose. By the end of their set, my sinuses are clear. *The Moseleys cured my cold.*

Next time, at Costa Mesa's Din Din at the Bamboo Terrace, I arrive in plenty of time, early enough to catch a painful sound check. The drums are fucking earsplitting. My photographer leaves quickly even though he has earplugs.

The show begins. Bunny asks fretfully, "What . . . key is that in?" Palmsley breaks a drumstick and hits someone in the audience with it. The Moseleys just might be the worst band in the whole world, but as they pound through one metal anthem after another, Harvey warns the women in the audience, "Don't listen too close; you might wake up pregnant!"

I know better than to love the Moseleys as I do. I am, after all, *not stupid.* But the weight of history is against me. When Pamela Des Barres pioneered the art of slutting after rock bands in the 1960s and 1970s, she was lighting the way for a million girls to shut up and put out. When Heather Locklear wore white leather to marry Tommy Lee—and after that, the enviably coifed Richie Sambora—she was acting out the fantasy of every heavy-metal high school girl. And ladies? Don't you want to grow up to be like Pamela Anderson? Even my own mother was not immune: in 1965, she spent a week showing tiny, charming Levon Helm the finer sights of Norman, Oklahoma, when he was touring with Bob Dylan and the Band. And she has carried a very small torch for him for almost forty years.

A few weeks later, Rex, Grady and Bunny pick me up by cab. In a blatant and successful attempt to garner some press, they are taking me to dinner at one of Sunset Beach's many pirate-themed restaurants. They are at the top of their game, wearing matching T-shirts and handing me something they've written and torn from a spiral notebook:

> *Oh, yeah, we're gonna get some! You got a rock & roll itch somewhere down there, and we're gonna scratch it. We're no dogs in the manger so don't ersatz us with no copycat acts who tryin' to bark up our tree! Only one band gonna heal that burning sensation, that fungus you went to see some mere mortal doctor for. . . . When you knew all along that the remedy was right there in your face. Straight on down the line you [the people] have been a carrier of the rock virus. Oh, yeah, we're gonna be a rock & roll bitch for you! We'll suck you dry! You ain't gonna need no soap when the sires of rock vengence [sic] lather you up and hose you down. You're gonna shoot your mouth off when we show you what those hole [sic] are for. . . .*
>
> *Love,*
> *The Moseley's [sic]*

They are so lame.

Bunny says, "You gotta keep the motor running."

Someone says, "Dude, you said, 'Keep the motor running.'"

Bunny becomes insecure. "Is that cool?" he asks.

Bunny talks about his infection, about ointments and applying them liberally to the infected area and repeating as needed.

Grady talks about his rock & roll vendetta. "It hasn't given us a fair shake in life. It's made us the cold-tempered people that we are. But we're opening up. We're looking for justice."

"And our vendetta," Bunny adds, helpfully.

"But we're not angry," says Grady.

"We're just saying hi," Bunny adds, helpfully.

Building Exterior, New York City, 1993

The grim façades of Alphabet City crumble before us. There, on Avenue B, is the Unconscious Collective, wherein actors perform a pseudoscientific, paranoid-conspiracy, serial comedy. The clean-cut young man starring as the professor is handsome in a scrawny, sandy way. But after the show, as he prepares to go home, he changes into his normal street clothes: blue tights; red spandex bikini; in-line skates; cape and helmet; and a big, yellow A on his chest. He is Amazing Man, and I am smitten. My eyes dilate, my skin reddens, my breath shortens and I pant. Here, clearly, is my mate.

A couple of weeks later, Amazing Man tells me he can't see me anymore: he has to go away for a while, for a "rest." His parents are sending him for help. I cry. He tells me I am an amazing woman. When someone with a yellow A on his chest tells you you are an amazing woman, it means a lot more than when a random, middle-management schmo in a bar says the same thing. Much, much more.

Amazing Man was my first rock-star love, even though to my knowledge he'd never picked up so much as an oboe. And that is one of the many glittering facets of rock-starness: you do not have to be Def Leppard to be a rock star. You can be the most preposterous high-school band ever to play a backyard kegger. You can be a bartender (especially a bartender) or a rodeo clown.

Honorary rock stars are everywhere. For Christ's sake, you can be a bank teller, as long as when you go out at night, you walk with your legs far apart to accommodate your low-swinging man meat, and you look deep into the eyes of the nearest girl and tell her pretty lies. And she will fall for it every time. Girls are very stupid.

Back at the restaurant, Bunny and Grady are showing off. "I don't know who I'm cooking an omelet for in the morning," boasts Grady, the dimpled one, before discussing breathable fabrics for one's nether regions.

Rex, meanwhile, has been playing with my small son for an hour now, teaching him to jab, and Bunny sees me watching. "Maybe the wedding band's not so bad right now," he cackles. Rex speaks for the first and only time. He calls literature "the primal experience."

Grady is talking about the Man. "The Man? He's this guy. We've never seen him."

Bunny is talking about how this restaurant offers all-you-can-eat bread sticks. Grady tells the waitress he doesn't eat red meat. "It causes colon cancer," he informs her helpfully.

They talk about their cornucopia of songs. There is "The Witch" and "Dungeon of Love." They've also got "a sexy little song called 'Jack the Ripper'" and one about how they just need Vitamin U.

"It's a multitude of cascading colors of songs. We're like a rainbow," somebody says.

The Moseleys love cocaine.

"We imagine it's beautiful!" Grady says.

"I haven't done it yet, but I would like to!" says Bunny. "We would like to do lines off chicks' asses!"

Rex plays with my son some more.

They are so lame, and it's all I can do not to rip off my skirt and let them do lines off my ass.

Like the popular e-mail that sorts women into personality types by what they order (beer: good; fruity, fancy drinks: high-maintenance; white zinfandel: clueless, but thinks she's sophisticated), you can tell a lot about a girl by the rock star she covets.

Drummers, though the butt of all their fellow musicians' jokes (they are endlessly mocked as grunting cavemen), get wild chicks who look at them and can picture nothing but what that ceaseless, pounding rhythm would be like in the sack.

Bassists get cool, slightly stand-offish girls who like them because they (bassists) are confident enough to let the singer get the attention while they (bassists) stand coolly still and smirk at the audience.

I don't know anyone who goes out with guitarists, though I'm sure there are a bunch.

Singers go out with women who think well enough of themselves to think they would look good in *People* Magazine. I don't know too many women who go out with singers: Could they ever love you as much as they love themselves?

There are women who have no set preference but fall recklessly in love with any and all of the above. I am one of these women. I can mock my girlfriends for being stupid enough to chase after rock stars. After all, I know better. But the flesh is weak.

Nobody goes out with maraca players.

After the first or seventeenth time a rock star has loved and dumped you without a word—and there you are thinking you're all crazy because you must have imagined that you and the rock star had a tendre going—you recognize the danger in these beautiful egomaniacs. You now know better than to get entangled with a rock star again. And you still know better, even as another rock star is looking deep into your eyes and you are surrendering for the second or eighteenth time.

How did you get this way? Back in 1977, you didn't need the actual Leif Garrett. It was enough to kiss his poster over the bed. But you didn't learn the lesson in this story of long-distance love through glossy facsimile: cherish rock stars from afar.

And after you have been loved and wordlessly dumped again—after showing up at gigs, happy and fluttery, while he was looking right through you—you'll start believing that you really are crazy and just made up the whole thing in your crazy, crazy head, which is obviously crazy. Even Pamela Anderson isn't as crazy as you because at least she wasn't imagining she was married to Tommy Lee.

Why do intelligent, attractive young women get suckered over and over by these no-good dirty dogs? It's a question we frequently whine among ourselves. There are as many answers as there are girls with cartoon hearts in thought bubbles over their heads. But there are a few general traits.

There is the fact that these boys are somewhat seedy, and so they must be sexually knowing. There is the sensitivity, hidden like a little boy's, that just needs mothering. There is the eye contact—lots and lots of eye contact. Like Irishmen, rock stars know the power of impaling you with a look. There is the power of the spotlight—any spotlight—which is why girls love their professors and their bartenders and their dentists, too. There is the hope that someday there will be reflected fame. And there is the tortured soul that needs only *you* for a balm.

You imagine you could be his Yoko. You imagine you could be his Vitamin U.

We Must Have Syph

By the time I got to my emergency doctor's appointment on Monday, I was ready to throw up. I'd had a pimple on my bits that had turned into a pustulent sore. Pustulence! Right there on my business! And now, thanks to a plotline on the Sunday night medical soap *Grey's Anatomy*, a show I greatly enjoy as all the sexy young doctors find time to pout at one another and roll out clever banter before rolling messily into bed, I'd figured out that the disturbing wound was syphilis.

By the time I went online and looked at images of syph, I was ready to cry and faint at the same time. I discreetly told my boss I was having a health issue and needed to take the rest of the day. Then, since any time I don't tell every single thought that's in my head I think I'm lying by omission, I told my boss's wife I was going to the doctor because I was pretty sure I had syphilis. But *then* I said, "Ha ha! I'm kidding! I don't really think I have syphilis!" I'm pretty sure that fooled her.

Syphilis is very treatable, and I'd caught it—I mean diagnosed it—nice and early, but I was still gonna have to have the "Um, it seems I have syphilis" talk with this one man I like, the man who'd undoubtedly given me syph. I would have to be really non-judgmental, but that would be the last I'd see of him. I remembered this one boyfriend who angrily told me I'd given him chlamydia, except when I went to the doctor—whoops!—I didn't have chlamydia. Boy, was his face red!

So either this man I like had given me syphilis and therefore would be too embarrassed ever to see me again (which might not be that bad, considering he'd given me *syphilis*!), or he would go to the doctor and find out he didn't have syphilis, and then I'd be the girl he was dating who had syphilis, or rather the girl he *had been* dating who had syphilis, and when you're talking about syphilis, chlamydia sounds positively adorable. God, I'd love to be able to say it was chlamydia. Prom queens get chlamydia. Old French whores (okay, and fabulous gay men—who should be using condoms) get syph; it's in a social disease class all its own. So, really, this talk I was going to have to have was a lose-lose. No good could come of it. I rehearsed it many times in my mind.

Ooh, la la! Romance!

Feet in the stirrups Monday afternoon, I explained, quavering, to the doctor about my syphilis.

"Oh, that's not syphilis," he said, poking at my tragic lymph nodes. "It looks like you cut yourself shaving."

Come to think of it, I *had* cut myself shaving. Right in that very spot!

"What kind of razor do you use?" he asked me.

Well, apparently, a razor with syph!

"I don't have syphilis," I told my boss. "It turns out I cut myself shaving." He was perplexed. "You cut yourself shaving and immediately thought you had *syphilis*?" he asked, as though that was somehow an unreasonable conclusion to draw. Well, of course. Wouldn't everybody?

I'm not generally a fearful person. I don't think I've ever been afraid for my physical safety in bad neighborhoods, even walking alone at night. And since the tsunami hit, I don't even give a second's thought to terrorism. Our 3,000 or so dead on 9/11 were a tragedy, but it sure wasn't Indonesia.

What I'm afraid of is losing the things I love.

I'm afraid of lung cancer, because I love to smoke. I'm afraid of breast cancer, because I love my bosoms. And I'm afraid of social diseases because I've had a tender, decades-long love affair with my cooter. It may not be the best cooter in the world—there are even plastic surgeons advertised in our very own *OC Weekly* who would snip it and clip it and stitch it up solid for me in the unholy name of cooter perfection—but it's the best cooter I've got, and it does me just fine. And it's why I don't believe in waxing either: Why would I give my lady pieces such pain?

So why again is the Reverend Lou Sheldon so afraid of gays? And Neal Horsley, the anti-abortion activist who blithely admits he used to fuck (actual) mules—what's he so afraid of exactly? Dude's an Orange Alert all by hisself!

I would never, ever violate a mule. But I also don't want my parts to fall off just because I like having sex. I'm a 32-year-old woman; it's not like I can *help* it.

I might not ever have sex again.

Unfortunately, I can't not ever have sex again: if I never have sex again, the cynical right-wing elite in this country will have won. And oh, yes, I'm afraid of that. I'm afraid of losing the country I love to an unholy alliance of wild-eyed, bigoty, *Handmaid's Tale* wack-jobs and a bunch of corporations that bridle the wack-jobs' social bizarrities for their own ends. The breathtakingly evil Priscilla Owen—who, thanks to the Senate centrists' Nuclear Option "compromise" is about to sit on our Fifth Circuit Court of Appeals—hasn't just legislated from the bench on abortion, she's also backed the defendants in just about every case ever brought by a plaintiff against an insurance company, health maintenance organization or corporation when a defective product blew up in someone's face, until even Alberto Gonzales, who wrote the memo justifying torture for the military that led to the abuses at Abu Ghraib, and who sat with her on the Texas Supreme Court, even *he* accused her of an "unconscionable act of judicial activism."

The corporations are happy, the wack-jobs are happy, and in the course of them taking away our constitutional right to address our grievances, we'll also be satisfying (for a minute) the unending demands of the burka crowd who are moving this country's discourse so far to the right (you should *see* some of the evangelicals' online rantings about transferring ownership of a woman from her daddy to her beau) that Zell Miller is starting to look like the civilized Left. No, sir, I challenge *you* to a duel!

The Family Research Council is speaking out against a possible vaccine for Human Papilloma Virus—the virus that causes genital warts and is a leading indicator in 250,000 cervical cancer deaths each year—because inoculating against cervical cancer would be a "license" for young women "to engage in premarital sex."

When it came time to find someone to oversee reproductive health for the Food and Drug Administration, we appointed an OB-GYN who won't prescribe birth control to unmarried women.

And abortions are up under George W. Bush, whose cohorts insist sex is only for the married—even though you *know* they only got married because they knocked someone up. (As a quick side-note to the sociologists who can't figure out why there's an "epidemic" of spinsterhood among college-educated career women: it's because we're too responsible to ever accidentally get pregnant. I love it when researchers can't figure out this common-sense shit—like when they were mystified as to why small women were so much more likely to be injured by their airbags. Duh. We have to sit really close to the steering wheel to get our feet to reach the pedals!)

But that's okay, because George W. Bush's abstinence-only education teaches that condoms fail one-third of the time.

Which is how, come to think of it, I got my imaginary syph.

Syph, of course, under George W. Bush, has skyrocketed. Chlamydia too, but chlamydia is just flat-out adorable.

If you don't get chlamydia, the right-wing terrorists have won.

Do you wanna dance?

"Well, it is certainly mature," my boy's teacher said, her brows raised in silent communiqué as if miming the location of the next safe house for handmaids, when I brought up the Judy Blume book that he and I'd been reading. She and I were both thinking of the wet-dream talk that comes—thank you!—after all of four pages.

I'd known Judy Blume was a godless whore—why do you think I liked her?—but four pages isn't much of a buffer when you start reading about sperm with your ten-year-old baby. "Do you know what a wet dream is?" I asked him, and he didn't, and now he does.

Ugh.

But my boy's teacher continued. "It's really up to parents to decide if their child is mature enough for her books. Judy," she twinkled, and with that small intimacy signaled her approval, although you might need a member of the Resistance to interpret the original encoded French, "has always been controversial."

And that's the happy state of life in one of the few OC classrooms that isn't yet handing out Communion or teaching in tongues: the encouragement to read something other than *Left Behind: The Executin'*, or that book the National Park Service sells at the Grand Canyon gift shop that says the gorge was carved by Noah's flood, may have to come in code, but come it does. But don't worry, fundie friends! They're singing lots of songs about Jesus, Our Savior and King, at this week's "holiday" program. Don't let the bastards grind you down.

My father, who is a Jew, and thus usually an informed person, had not the faintest inkling that a Bette Midler show would be full of the gays. "Gay guys?"

he asked, with the same faux-shock with which you'd say "There's traffic on the 5?" except that shocked he actually was when I explained the reason the Pond was packed (on a Tuesday!) was that all the gay guys had come down from LA, where Midler wasn't playing a date. "Nobody's coming down from LA," he pooh-poohed. "You came down from LA," I reminded him. He had no idea the woman whose album *The Divine Miss M* he'd proclaimed the Album of the Seventies had started her career as Bathhouse Betty. He didn't even realize that everybody to whom I'd mentioned my father's Bette Midler fandom had asked whether my father was one of the boys in the band.

"No," I kept explaining, "he's a hippie and a Jew."

But walking through the Pond, my father actually began to point at the queers. "There's one!" he said. Pointing. "Oh, there's another! But of course you knew that, with your history of faghaggery."

He almost made it sound as though my days of faghaggery were done and gone.

And for those of you who pooh-pooh the Divine Miss Midler, which is pretty much any straight under sixty, you must realize that before she emoted "Wind Beneath My Wings," she was a completely inspirational, foul-mouthed freak who mostly sang boogie and big band.

Behind a huge screen painted with the *very* Tom of Finland *The Fleet's In* by Paul Cadmus (the original, a beautiful mess of sailor booty, showed at the Orange County Museum of Art a few years back) were Midler's band and her tutu-ed backup girls, and Midler arrived in satin sailor suit and Shirley Temple curls flying in on a giant carousel horse. Gay? But *oui!* And my dad and I and every Jew and old lady in the place loved every second. Not to mention the queers.

So she's hilarious, and she talks like a trucker, and for God's sake, she's fifty-nine and was tap-dancing for an *hour*—while she was singing—and my dad loved nothing better than the *ancient* Catskills jokes she was doing (which were older than the Raiders' offensive line), but she updated lots, too, for the young men in the house, with lots of jokes about Britney and Christina and watching the particular trash that is Ms Aguilera strutting around in a g-string and pasties covering her nipples— pasties and a g-string!—and does Ms M get even one word of thanks?

The second half of the show was mostly retreads—the famous mermaid-in-a-wheelchair routine goes on for an awfully long time, with lots of different fish puns, and the Catskills and the Bush jokes, and the jitterbugging, and the full raw mouth—but at the end of the show, Pink showed up to sit in on "The Rose." And if you've ever wondered if Pink knows the words to "The Rose"? Yes. Despite that somewhat beefy appearance, she does. Toward the end of the show (after, I think, "Wind Beneath My Wings"—and no, cool kittens, I don't like it either, but I suppose it has to be done—and right before a scorching "Do You Wanna Dance?"), there was a particularly touching homage to Mr Rogers. With the beloved children's show host singing on a screen (I'm not at all appalled by it like I was with ghoulish Natalie Cole positively eating her dead dad), Midler delivered a lovely counterpoint during a very poignant "I Like to Be Told." They like to be told if it'll hurt or it won't, and they like to be told when you're coming home. It's such a simple plea for honesty; they can handle it, if you'll tell them, but they really want to know.

Of course, I'm pretty sure I cured my son of that once and for all.

DeLay Lady Lay (Lay across my Big Partisan Fundie Conservative Ethically Compromised Brass Bed)

My little brother Cakeyboy and I were in the car on Saturday when he came up with the funnest game *ever.* . . . Or Kevin Federline?

It goes like this: Flavor Flav or Kevin Federline?

The Nuge or Kevin Federline?

Kobe Bryant or Kevin Federline?

Trent Lott or Kevin Federline?

The fugitive-rapist Max Factor heir or Kevin Federline?

George W. Bush or Kevin Federline?

Michael Moore or Kevin Federline?

Andy Dick or Kevin Federline?

For the record, there are few people in this world so grotesque that I wouldn't choose a night with them over a night with the sweaty sac of Britney Spears' grubby hubby, but Tom DeLay and, naturally, Andy Dick (okay, and Michael Moore: I don't do fatties) managed to make the cut.

How icky is Tom DeLay? Isn't *ickier than Kevin Federline* saying enough?

Well, no. Probably not.

Okay: imagine this icky image, which I found while cruising (get it?) *Salon.* "He's going through the same thing I went through," [Trent] Lott told the *Chronicle*, vis-à-vis the embattled Congressman DeLay, who really has had just one hell of a couple of weeks. "If you are a conservative Republican leader from the South . . . strap it on, baby, because you are fixing to get it."

Can somebody help me with what Mr Senator Lott might have been trying to say? Because I'm not sure I can wrap my puny mortal brain around it. A helmet? A gun, maybe? Strap on a gun? That's what I'm hoping he meant: a giant gun, with lots of bullets hanging from one of those sexy bandolero strappy jobs, like the sexy bandolero strappy job on that sexy wee human Sylvester Stallone as John Rambo, and not, say, a giant dildo like the thing from *Seven*, which is what it sounds like he was talking about, but that would be wrong. There's lots of places—and I believe Congressman DeLay's home state of Texas is one of them, and now that I've Googled it, I find that as usual I'm right—where dildos are illegal, so I hope that wasn't what old Trent had in mind.

You heard it here first: Trent Lott, in addition to pining for the good old days of segregation, advocates getting reamed with illegal, obscene devices. In men's bottoms!

You know who else likes to think about men's bottoms? You're so smart! It's our old friend the Reverend Lou! Have the Reverend Lou and his Traditional Values Coalition yet condemned the graphic and unpleasant language of Lott (R-Ass)? No, not that I can figure. But I like to picture him picturing it.

"But Commie Girl," you're muttering into your beard, causing the little blobs of dried rice to wiggle and sway in a most unpleasant manner, "what the fuck is with your hard-on for Tom DeLay? What has he ever done to you and your liberal media cohorts that you cackle in malevolent glee just because he's had a few little slip-ups?" Listen, Hugh Hewitt! I don't have to explain myself to you! Just know that following his rejiggering of the Ethics Committee (replacing the *Republicans* who'd voted to censure him three times in the past year with some fellows who'd contributed to his legal defense fund); his alleged money laundering of corporate contributions (as Molly Ivins says, it's hard to run afoul of campaign finance law in Texas, seeing as how they've just got the one) through not just his political action committees, but his children's foundation as well; his wife pulling in a couple hundred large from lobbyists for "long-term strategic guidance"; his cushy foreign travel paid for by some Russian thugs; and his general dour demeanor and bad hair, well, we just don't like him. It has absolutely nothing to do with his scorched-earth/flat-earth calls to subvert the Constitution and replace checks and balances and the independent judiciary because even though a majority of judges have been appointed by Republican presidents—and in Bush vs Gore, returned the favor—once in a while they *still* say we can't execute minors or torture people at Gitmo, and, damn it, for DeLay that kind of heathen judicial activism just won't stand!

Did someone say "heathen"? It was probably the Dominionists, DeLay's fellow travelers who want a pledge to Jesus Christ, our crucified savior, recited every morning in homeroom. DeLay's also blamed Columbine on the teaching of evolution and expressly calls for the US to be run as a "Christian nation" on "biblical principles," which sounds nice till it's your turn to collect the stones for the adulterers—not to mention the sodomites.

Saturday night, I threw Suparna the Rocket Scientist in the car and headed up to Santa Monica for a party celebrating painter Stephen Douglas' big-ass house. The party, thrown by Douglas' special lady (photographer E.F. Kitchen) was fab, and the house, she was big. We hung out with Orange County's Best Artist Jorg Dubin and his young friend (but not in a gay way) Jeff Peters. We ate food. We drank drinks. And eventually, the party was over and they made us leave. It was time to hit someplace young, and fancy, and sexy. We hit the Brig, a fancy, sexy, young place that's great for when you want an $8 well drink while you're being ignored. Suparna, now schnockered, didn't like it, filled as it was with 24-year-olds who not only were not properly enthralled by us but in fact had a disturbing tendency to turn away smack in the middle of a sentence. And I was even wearing a slutty frock!

I dragged her away. "We're going to the Roosterfish," I said. "We're getting some boyfriends if it kills us (softly)." Venice's premier gay bar would be our Ground Zero.

By the time we stumbled out of the Roosterfish at 2:15, we couldn't beat the gay boys off with their sticks. Did they love us? Did they tell us how beautiful we are, and how much they liked our slutty frock, and my goodness, we're so smart? Did they wrap themselves around us like we were Madonna and they were our little Red Strings?

All that was missing was Trent Lott, a strap-on and the good Reverend Lou.

The Boy Who Felt me Up at the Canyon inn

It has come to my attention that some of our more conservative friends are somewhat—hmmm, how to maintain my usual courtly *politesse*?—ignorant and retarded. Not retarded in a lovey, nice, sweet way like a retarded adult you might see in the grocery store, holding onto his dear father's hand. In fact, scratch *retarded* completely. Let's make it ignorant and *dick-mouthed* instead. But not dick-mouthed in a fun, liberated, gay way. More like in the insano, toxically repressed way of the Right Reverend Lou Sheldon. You know: like someone who's got a mouth full of dick!

But what is bringing out these terrible unkindnesses from between my gentle lips?

Well, we at *OC Weekly* HQ have been bombarded with idiots these past few days, threatening, among other things, to have our paper "shut down" and, um, "kill [us]." I mean, *I* haven't because as you might imagine, I'm pretty well universally beloved, but my tall, urbane editor? He's been fielding phone calls from lunatics like he's Ann Coulter's on-call shrink.

Where shall I begin, my pets? (A) We don't shut down papers that disagree with the gubmint in the United States of America; we leave that to Paul Bremer and the freedom-bringers of the Coalition Provisional Authority calling the shots (get it?) from one of Saddam's lovely and tasteful palaces. And (B) What's with all you victims who say you're being *harmed* by someone's *opinion*? Weren't you just yesterday ranting about the liberal pansies—and their idiotic political correctness—who were supposed to be the victim brigade? Or was that before all the coloreds and feminazis started beating you out for college admission slots? I'm always amused—actually, no I'm not—at the way our friends on the

Right shriek stuff about us when they do the exact same thing but worse. *Par exemple*: Bill Clinton was castigated for years for Travelgate—he fired some people in the White House Travel Office so he could appoint some cronies— and for looking at White House appointees' FBI files. But Valerie Plame's file wasn't just looked at—the Bush administration outed her as an undercover CIA agent to get even with her longhaired-hippie-freak of a diplomat husband's not swearing the Loyalty Oath to Bush adviser Karl Rove. Even more recently, a White House schnauzer huffed that John Kerry was "beyond the bounds of acceptable discourse" for saying at a black church, "The Scriptures say, what does it profit, my brother, if someone says he has faith but does not have works?" before out-of-boundsily continuing, "When we look at what is happening in America today, where are the works of compassion?" Funny, the White House saying all this religion talk is out of bounds—while the *National Catholic Reporter* (*NCR*) published this tidbit this week: "A Vatican official told *NCR* June 9 that in his meeting with Cardinal Angelo Sodano and other Vatican officials, [President] Bush said, 'Not all the American bishops are with me' on the cultural issues. The implication was that he hoped the Vatican would nudge them toward more explicit activism."

Like denying John Kerry, you and me Holy Communion! Me, I'm not even pro-choice, and I still wouldn't be able to receive the holy cracker—being pro-gay-marriage is godless enough to deny me my sacred rites as far as our not-Catholic president is concerned, while he's busy deciding dogma for the Holy See. Jesus, am I still talking? Talk, talk, talk!

So there we were at the Canyon Inn, and Long Tall Gina had found a victim. Very soon, she would make her cry—at least, according to Gina.

"All my friends tell me I got really screwed in the divorce," Blondie was reputedly whining before later saying as Gina gave her a ride home, "Oh, you live in the ghetto part of Anaheim Hills . . . comparatively speaking." Anyway, it seems that she only gets $5,000 per month in alimony—plus the 700 grand cash settlement—and that this is something to feel *deprived* about. Gina, while long and tall and unmitigatedly hot, is not generally a good shoulder for cryin'. She told her to get off her ass and do something with her life, called her an uneducated floozy, and suggested she tell men she was a waitress or whatever else she wanted to tell them, as long as she didn't tell them she had $700,000 in the bank or she might—inconceivably, I know—attract *fortune hunters*. "That's happened to me twice!" gasped Blondie—who was actually really, really nice, but c'mon! "*What are the odds?*" Gina screamed at her with her patented lacerating sarcasm. And the lady sobbed.

But you wanted to hear about the 21-year-old who felt me up. And so do I! So there he was. He was 21. And he had that soft, floppy hair that's so cute on the Absolut Hunk. And he was 21. We started to chat. What did he do? "I work with special-ed kids," said he, oozing not-lyingness. Honey, I know it works on most of your pretty victims, but I was born a lot less yesterday than you were. I laughed! *Ha,* ha, ha, ha! So what did he do for real? He's working on a satirical novel about World War II. We talked long and hard about Joseph Heller ("Are you funny?" I asked him. "No," he said. "Satire doesn't have to be funny." Oh, like Dennis Miller! Then he explained that his work is more in the vein of Orwell, "like 1982," to which I replied, "1984 is hilarious—to smart people"), and as I opined and deconstructed and lectured and opined some more, he never took his eyes from mine and seemed to follow right along as his right hand crept to my left breast. Hey, hey! I'm talking here!

Still, it was smooth, except that it most certainly and preposterously was not.

I pulled myself to my greatest five-foot-two and froze him to pieces with my patented icy, affronted-Southern-lady glare.

"What are you drinking?" I chirped, and then I bought him one like the sad, old, sugar mama I will someday be.

paging john ashcroft

Say you happen to be at a wedding so Republican that Karen Hughes, the woman who gave us George W. Bush, has flown in from Texas to give one of the readings. (From the Book of Ruth, actually, one of my faves—you know, "Whither thou goest, I shall go," etc. It's a terribly romantic bit of Old Testament and more nuptially hopeful than Leviticus 20:10: "If [there is] a man who commits adultery with another man's wife, one who commits adultery with his friend's wife, the adulterer and the adulteress shall surely be put to death.") Now say that you are pretty much the only person at this elegant and heartfelt union who is—how shall we put it?—French. By which I mean not French, but communist.

Then you should be very, very careful not to say to the junior bridesmaids (from Dallas, no less!) while showing them how to dance to Van Halen, "You just kind of make a stupid face. You know, like you're on drugs!"

You and your moral relativism will be reported to Attorney General John Ashcroft *immediately.*

Now, it doesn't matter if you realize your mistake faster than you can say "public lynching." What you've just done is the equivalent of saying *hell* to an old Southern lady—which, we learned one night in Jackson, just ain't done.

And it doesn't matter that you're making fun of heavy-metal freaks by saying they have the same stupid face you might see on people who use drugs—that you're not actually recommending drugs or their use. You have said *drugs* to nice girls from Texas.

And it doesn't matter that you blurt out, "Not that any of you would ever do drugs." There's no damage control now. You have said *bomb* on an airplane. Would you care to make a Hitler joke in a Miami convalescent home now?

"I need to get a drink of water," the oldest and most glamorous of the quartet will intone prettily (and Dallas preteens can be glamorous indeed) before leading her charges off the dance floor and over to the chaperones, who have clearly (and successfully) coached this young lady in how to deal with peer pressure and iffy situations—iffy situations like you. "Talk to your kids about drugs," say the ads. "They'll listen."

Clearly the Office of National Drug Control Policy is right on target about this; clearly it works; and just as clearly, you have just been reported. You are being watched. You are the Jerk at the Wedding—the Jerk that in better days you used to smirk and titter at and gossip about—and you're so mortified with yourself you could just about catch Ebola and die right there, bleeding from all your bits. Ann Coulter, Miss Social Graces herself, could shriek that you're a scandalous traitor, and she'd be right. Ass.

Also, whatever you do? Don't say *ass*.

Kids Korner!

Ass, ass, ass, ass, ass.

Ass.

A Tender Moment

Feeling like an embarrassed bit of toejam plucked from the un-American foot of the Green (Communist) Party, I headed home to the kid. The party had been lovely, the weekend perfect, the wedded couple beautiful and touching, but I was subdued. Am I a bad mother, a slob, a moral relativist? Am I inappropriate and vulgar with children? Do I not give My Little Buttercup the guidance he needs to grow into a fine citizen, a fine man?

I pondered this still while we smoked some family crack.

No, I decided. I'm fine.

Then I sent the boy to buy more crack. Frankly, I don't like to go to the crack dealer's house myself since it's pretty sketchy and gross. But since Jimmy turned nine, it's about time he pulled his own weight.

"Mom," said my buttercup with his usual wit and hilarity. "Please don't make me go buy crack anymore."

Kids say the darndest things!

SECTION FOUR

Political Football

Capitol Punishment

How I stopped worrying and learned to love Arnold Schwarzenegger

I was already back home from three days in Sacramento when Jennifer in the governor's press office called about my credential.

"We were only able to find two articles where you actually covered the governor at an *event*," she said.

That meant that someone in the governor's press office had waded through the twenty-three Nexised stories where I've written about Arnold Schwarzenegger in order to find the two where I'd actually seen him in person. And that meant that the goodly folks in the governor's press office had gotten an eyeful of stories like this one:

> When Arnold Schwarzenegger talks, I listen. Well, I mean, sometimes I listen. Sometimes I just stare off into space and wonder what would happen if you put a cheeseburger in front of Maria Shriver. Or a plump baby. Actually, come to think of it, I really don't listen at all.

Or:

> Arnold Schwarzenegger is elected governor of the golden dream by the sea. He reneges on every campaign promise he can remember making, and then reneges on other candidates' promises for good measure. Everyone is thrilled to pieces and blames the legislature, except Congressman Dana Rohrabacher (R-The Taliban), who blames Bill Clinton.

Here's one:

> A sex scandal could never sink our good Governor Schwarzenegger, though not for his lack of trying. And I'd still sleep with him before I slept with Kevin Federline, though I have to say: not *happily*."

And here's my personal fave:

> Hey, you know who's charming? Arnold Schwarzenegger! He's so charming! I think it's especially charming how the emcees at his events goad the mobs to "find the guy from the *Los Angeles Times* and beat him up!" Ha! That is hilarious! It is so very funny—especially when you consider how very easy it is to sway and incite the kinds of folk who would show up for an Arnold rally. By which I mean they are simple-minded and stupid. Thank you.
>   Hey, here's a funny one the emcees should try: "Find the shops of the Jews and break all the windows, and in the morning, we will round them up and put them on the trains! Ha, ha, just kidding!" Thank you. You know what's even more charming than that? How Arnold grabs the breasts of the women and says to them, "Have you ever had a man slide his tongue up your ass?" and all of these things. No, I'm not bothering to put *allegedly*.
>   Sue me.

I've always found that one to be especially well-put!

"It'll be you trying to get an interview with the governor," my editor was saying. "It'll be great!"

It would not be great. Do you really think Arnold Schwarzenegger's people will let him be interviewed by any media besides talk radio demagogues John & Ken? And even if he was the free-and-easy open-government type—and even if he wasn't now so sought after by the media that he has to hold his pressers in the Convention Center—do you really think they'd let him get within a hundred yards of *me*? Now, with Schwarzenegger's approval ratings sliding to

Bush-like lows, and the media licking its chops in slavering glee, I can't even get Schwarzenegger's guy on the phone—a guy I've known for probably three years now, a guy near whom I've attended weddings and funerals and brisses (actually, not funerals and brisses).

And what if the governor tried to touch my boobs? If the governor said something about his tongue and my bottom, and I decked him in his oversized noggin, would I go to jail?

Still, I love Sacramento, being a total power slut and all, and the city itself is just flat gorgeous. Have you ever seen the Capitol park in spring? No? Don't you *want* to fall in love? I started to warm to the discomfiting idea. I could hang out with my favorite communist state senator, Gil Cedillo, who is sexy, like Al Pacino, and is a communist!

"Just so you know," my boss told me, "I'm not sending you up there to hang out with Gil Cedillo. You're going up there to work."

Oh.

Forty-five minutes after I'd checked into my hotel, I was sucking down an Absolut rocks (with a twist) at Chops, formerly the venerable Brannan's. It still has the dark woods and orchids, but they've evicted the Pat Brown posters and the sad, defeatist "George McGovern: It's Time We Won."

This was my grand scheme: to dine at the places the governor might dine (Chops, Frank Fat's and the Esquire Grill) and ambush him with my delightfulness. I would be polite, certainly, while asking such brain-ticklers as "Knowing what you now do about the state of the budget, and how the shortfall could not have been easily made up, as you'd said it would, by forensic accounting to eliminate waste and fraud, would you still have supported your predecessor Gray Davis' recall?" and he would enjoy knocking brains with me. Clearly, going through his office was going to be an embarrassing waste of time for everyone involved.

But I bet I could find him at Chops.

I don't find him at Chops. But I'm having a delightful conversation with a teachers' union lobbyist about pensions and tenure—nobody's all that het up about Schwarzenegger's plan to raise the requirement for tenure from two years to five, the only part of his education proposal, which he's been trying to put on the ballot, still standing—and am soon being circled by legislative staffers in sharp suits and former Jerry Brown appointees. I don't think Sacramento has very many girls.

Schwarzenegger is on everyone's lips; even unseen, people are giddy about him, even if it's giddy with bristling hate. Everyone talks about him, everywhere I go.

It wasn't the same with Gray Davis.

Recently termed-out Senate President John Burton holds court in a corner but leaves before I see him. I nearly cry when someone tells me he'd been there. Lovely, foul-mouthed John Burton! Here's the *LA Times* when Burton was termed out from the Senate: "To protest what he considered Republican political attacks on the poor, he once drafted legislation that would have made it a crime to have an income below the poverty level. Another Burton bill would have required that state orphanages serve gruel."

Fuckin' John Burton, man. He's all right.

Wednesday afternoon, lateish: Tammy, Chops' gorgeous mid-thirties barkeep, says, "Well, when the governor was in here Monday night . . ."

"But I was here Monday night!" I say, outraged.

"Yeah, you were hanging out with Juan and those guys, right?"

"Yeah!"

"Well, he was downstairs."

Chops, it seems, has a downstairs.

Shit.

You have to understand about Schwarzenegger: with what is by all reports an obsessively focused mind and a fairly middle-of-the-road approach, he could actually be one of the great governors in history, à la Pat Brown—the man who built the University of California system and the freeways, who made California the destination for the entire country—and for a minute after his election, it looked like he might.

Sure, he was carried into office with only 48 percent of the vote on some fat lies (the California Republican Party was whipping up the always latent hate for Gray Davis by blaming him for the "energy crisis" when it was Republicans Curt Pringle and Pete Wilson who'd allowed their buddies at Enron to mug us in the first place)—and when his main competitors were Larry Flynt, Tom McClintock, Cruz Bustamante and pint-sized *Diff'rent Strokes* star Gary Coleman. And Schwarzenegger's campaign promises were legendary for the speed at which he broke them: not needing to fundraise from special interests, since he had his own private fortune (he quickly eclipsed Gray Davis, who liked to fundraise all day and all of the night, like the sad little pudding he was), or his vow to find the real groper just as soon as the election was over and done, or insuring all of California's needy children, or that he'd be able to balance our budget with just a bit of forensic accounting to ferret out waste and fraud—as my colleague Steve Lowery says, as if there's some $12 billion state fund somewhere that buys wigs for pre-op trannies, and once we just find it, poof! The budget's balanced!—before borrowing $8 billion to add to our deficit.

But when he was deal-making with Democrat John Burton—while the Republicans gnashed their teeth in the wilderness—the star-struck Burton was actually giving up quite a bit. It was a masterful bit of triangulation—and bipartisanship—on Schwarzenegger's part.

He changed, of course—or maybe flip-flopped. It was at the Republican National Convention in New York City that Arnold left behind his taste for cigar-fueled deal-making and got a sip of the possibilities of One Party Rule. He seemed carried away by the testosterone wing of the Republican Party, the wing that believes fighting fair is for pussies, that you do what it takes to win at all costs—including shutting down the Miami Dade recount through screaming, pounding intimidation or, as Arnold so famously did, intimidating a bodybuilding opponent by bagging his wife and then calling him up with her still in his bed.

He's always stomped right over his friends—witness his announcement of his candidacy for governor on Jay Leno's show, next to a publicly humiliated Richard Riordan: Riordan, who had already announced, had gone with him to the taping after Schwarzy had told him his announcement would be his endorsement of Riordan. Schwarzenegger had called soulfully for a new, bipartisan way of dealing with the Democratic Legislature, but after the Republican convention, that was gone in the blink of a roving eye.

All of a sudden anyone who disagreed with him wasn't an honest opponent but a "girly man" (snooze), and Arnold was no longer trying to find a middle way but was going to use his stardom and bully pulpit to push through devastating attacks on the poor, the middle class, small business and the four most respected professions in our state. Still, we did get that refund on our car tax.

Tuesday morning I don my chic business attire of mismatched separates and power-walk up to the Capitol. I stop in the governor's office first and ask for Stutzman. Here's Stutzman last time I saw him, not even a month ago maybe, during the Santa Ana leg of the governor's tour of woefully middlebrow eateries while trying to rock his proposals to cut police widows off the state pension plan:

Me: Hey, Stutzman!

Stutzman: Hey! Ha, ha!

Me: I wanna come up to Sacramento and see you guys!

Stutzman: Yeah, come up and see us!

Me: Can I get some time with the governor?

Stutzman: No. But come up and see us!

Me: What, see you through a window?

The receptionist gives me Veronica's number; Veronica will set up a coffee with Stutzman.

Veronica will never set up a coffee with Stutzman.

My work there done, I stop by the offices of Todd Spitzer (R-Anaheim or something), Tom Umberg (D-Anaheim) and Joe Dunn (D-Santa Ana). Spitzer's lady tells me I *definitely* won't be able to buy him lunch; it's Caucus Day! "Why don't you go ahead and ask him and see what he says?" I say, firm but nice. Peace through strength! Trust but verify! She calls an hour or two later. Definitely no. "Can I take him for a cup of coffee?" I ask. "I'm here till Thursday!" Her voice has an italics-laden edge now. *"He said, 'No, thank you.'"*

Damn. I want to see the governor? I can't even see Todd Spitzer.

I go hang out in Gil Cedillo's office for the rest of the morning, leisurely reading the newspaper in the office of Dan Savage (no relation to the sex columnist), who is Cedillo's chief of staff, while Cedillo's staffers take one constituent call after another.

"How am I?" one staffer says into her phone. "Well, I've been called a bitch and a child molester today, so not too hot."

Cedillo, surprisingly, is against child molestation, though you can't blame people for assuming he's not, seeing as he's so communist and all.

I thumb through the lobby copy of *The Nation* while some Concerned Women of America come in to lobby for Bill "I Love My Dead Gay Son!" Morrow's defense-against-fag-marriage bill. (For the record, Bill Morrow's son isn't dead; nor, most likely, does he love him.) They have very thick ankles.

Tuesday, noon: I get my nails done.

Tuesday, 1:30ish: I run into Gil Cedillo at the Capitol metal detector.
"Will you have dinner with me tonight?" I ask him in my breathiest, most charming voice.

His eyes scan for a second as he schedules in his head. "I would *love* to," he growls all sexy (like a communist Al Pacino), once his mental schedule's checked.

Tuesday, 2 or so: Esquire Grill. Fabulous chicken pasta. No governor in sight.

He's kind of like the Great and Powerful Oz, I think, if Dorothy had never actually tried to find him.

Schwarzenegger's audiences aren't quite as handpicked as the president's: he does actually venture forth in public, in venues where people haven't had to swear a loyalty oath to get in (seriously, at the president's "public" town hall meetings, you have to swear a loyalty oath)—although there was that one nurse who was escorted from a screening of *Be Cool* that the governor and his flunkies were attending, despite the fact that she had a ticket, because she was wearing her scrubs.

And true, he never actually enters a place through the front door (his handlers, paranoid and arrogant Pete Wilson people all, know better than to let him get his picture taken in front of screaming and angry PTA moms). But when you see him, it's exciting.

His star power was enough at various Republican conventions to get the types of true believers who actually attend—rabidly pro-life/anti-gay/put-prayer-back-everywhere-they-can-squeeze-it—to howl with love despite his social liberalism and refusal to get sucked into the Culture War.

But Schwarzenegger's handlers and advisers, remember, were formerly the handlers and advisers to Pete Wilson, who barely eked out two terms as governor. Try as they may, they are not Karl "Bush's Brain" Rove, but that's not stopping them from using the classic Rove tactic of hitting the opposition where it's strongest, thus neutralizing what should be its winningest points—see war hero John Kerry losing to an AWOL draft dodger, while the Swift Boat Vets screamed that his Silver Star, Bronze Star V, and *three* Purple Hearts were falsified, and that he shot himself in his own leg (before shooting a fleeing, naked child in the back) to get out of the country.

John Kerry the war hero becomes John Kerry the cowardly war criminal. And nurses, teachers, cops and firefolk become union tools, while PTA moms become special interests.

So far, it's backfiring: Schwarzenegger's approval ratings have dropped to 40 percent in the face of a $5 million barrage of teachers' union ads featuring pissed-off moms explaining (clearly and concisely, in the most effective political ad I've ever seen) that Schwarzenegger borrowed $2 billion from education and then broke his word and declined to pay it back. This, the mothers explain (not teachers, as they could be written off as—you guessed it!—union tools), shortchanges every classroom by $25,000. That's a lot!

But beating up on nurses and cops isn't the endgame, no matter how many times Schwarzenegger brags that he's kicking the nurses' asses: the endgame is forcing the unions to spend their money protecting themselves from raids on classrooms and their old-age security, negotiated in good faith back when we believed old people shouldn't have to live on cat food—and then the unions will have nothing left for whatever's next to come down the pike.

The endgame is Son of Paycheck Protection, a homegrown OC initiative from one of our more charming Machiavellis, Jim Righeimer, that would have castrated unions by forcing them to hold a vote with their members every time the leadership wanted to contribute to a campaign. So while Schwarzenegger's raised $26 million last year alone from the insurance industry and HMOs and energy companies—like Enron—little folks wouldn't be able to band together to match that kind of money.

Because unions are special interests, but Enron is not.

I call Veronica. She was just going to call me! Stutzman definitely doesn't have time for coffee—I've picked the week when the governor's budget revise is coming out, for one, and also the week when famed union organizer Miguel Contreras is being laid to rest following a heart attack at the heartbreakingly young age of fifty-two; since all the Dems will be in LA for his funeral, there is no session on Thursday so all the legislators will be gone any second as well—but Stutzman is going to call me. On my phone! Veronica says.

Veronica is a dirty liar.

I meet up with Tom Umberg. He asks after my small buttercup of a son, even remembering from my column that his name is "Buttercup" (man's got skillz!), and kisses judiciously the ass of Helen, the ancient Latina who runs the private Lege-only elevator. Helen tells us the governor's uncle was in the Capitol yesterday, and she took such good care of him, everyone said so! She even asked him if he would like to go see the Holocaust pictures on the second floor.

"You asked the governor's uncle if he would like to see the Holocaust exhibit?" we ask slowly. "Um, what did he say?"

"He said no," she tells us with a shrug.

Imagine that.

It's pretty early for Chops. I go anyway. Absolut on the rocks, with a twist. Okay: four.

Dinner with Gil Cedillo, Tuesday, lateish: We talk about sexy, sexy things. Mostly, the illegal alien driver's license bill, which Cedillo's been working on for seven years now. It's passed the Lege and was signed into law by Gray Davis in a blatant pander to the Latino community. It was Davis's downfall. Cedillo worked a deal with Schwarzenegger too, but Schwarzenegger reneged.

Imagine that.

Cedillo is going to be on the live broadcast of *The Al Franken Show* at the Crest Theater the next morning. I'd planned to go too!

Sigh.

Wednesday morning, at the Crest, a grand rococo theater of gilt and fleurs-de-lis, of peacock feathers and jewels, more than nine hundred people have arrived before 9 a.m. to see Al Franken. Security isn't making any of the lurkers sit, and Kelly DiGiacomo, the nurse who was evicted from *Be Cool* because she was wearing her scrubs—and so was clearly some kind of terrorist threat—is handed a tiara and full-blown orange roses fresh from someone's garden.

This is *much* nicer than trying to interview the governor.

Phil Angelides (he's the California state treasurer, people; get with it!) comes onstage. He's adorable, in a wonky Jew way. Is he Jewish? I don't know! Next to me is a representative from the Association of Flight Attendants, who lost her pension yesterday when a bankruptcy judge okayed United's reneging on labor contracts signed in good faith years ago. She's a little frazzled.

The organizers of the show, seeing my notebook and chic business attire of mismatched separates, escort my new friend and me to the front row. This is good, as it will enable Gil Cedillo, once his segment comes on, to see me stalking him.

Sigh.

But Angelides is a regular showstopper: he talks about Schwarzenegger's speech to the Republican National Convention, the one where he said he'd been inspired by Richard Nixon to enter politics.

"I too was inspired to enter politics by Richard Nixon," Angelides says, and his deadpan timing is impeccable. I'm telling you, people: comedy gold!

He talks about the financial cap Schwarzenegger's placed on the UC system, how $100 million has been cut from inner city outreach alone.

And he talks about shareholders' rights, and not investing California's multi-billion-dollar pension funds in companies that incorporate in a post office box overseas. But the governor, who's been losing his ass this year over privatizing pensions the way the president wants to privatize Social Security, hasn't made a peep about pension losses from the corporate scandals at Enron and AIG.

I regret a recent column where my big punchline regarding the coming governor's race was, "But who's gonna beat him? Phil Angelides?" Clearly Angelides is feeling pretty good about his chances. But a year's more like a dog year in politics, and Schwarzenegger's a ruthless prick.

Now, I'm not the world's best political prognosticator: I called the governor's race for Tom McClintock, and John Kerry by 340-something electoral votes.

But while all the mainstream media is reveling in Schwarzenegger's precipitous recent poll drop—not because they're liberal, but because they'd all bought the myth about his invincibility, so a drop is news, news, news!—I'm not nearly so silly as to think Schwarzenegger couldn't win handily on name ID alone no matter how pissed off at him the nurses (and teachers, and cops, and firefighters) are.

Still, at least Angelides, look-Jew though he does, isn't a stiff in the Gray Davis/Cruz Bustamante vein. If people saw him, they'd like him. Really, he's adorable!

And then Arnold would go on *John & Ken* to remind people the Mexicans are coming, and that would be that.

Behind me, a nurses' lobbyist tells me that, while the Dems will be attending the Rosary for Miguel Contreras in Los Angeles tonight, their fellow Catholic Schwarzenegger will be attending a fundraiser at the Bonadelle Mansion in Fresno. Shit. Now I have to rent a car and drive to *Fresno*.

I do not rent a car and drive to Fresno.

But I do contemplate it—all five hours' round trip. To Fresno. And just in case I ever rent that car and drive to Fresno, I decide to go to the governor's office and get my ass credentialed, something I might have thought about doing the first day if I wasn't already drunk. Like Brit-Brit and K-Fed, we're gonna make it official!

Did I have a press credential from law enforcement? Jennifer in the governor's press office wants to know. "We don't need them in Orange County," I reply, neglecting to mention I'd blown off my appointment with the sheriff's lady who was all ready to give me one some weeks ago.

I don't even carry business cards.

Do I cover the governor on a regular basis?

Oh, yes.

At events?

Um, sure.

Jen would call me; I needn't call her. Then, on Tuesdays and Thursdays between noon and 2 p.m., I could get my photo taken by the California Highway Patrol in Room 1160.

Keith in the CHP office is terribly helpful, even though he can't actually help.

I await Jen's call at a reception for Al Franken on the *Delta King* on Sacramento's peaceful chocolate river, having walked a couple of miles in my business attire of mismatched separates and some non-sensible (okay: hookery) shoes. I do not bother trying to meet Al Franken, who is stomping bowlegged through the small reception, shrimp already traveling from hand to mouth, like a very small Godzilla. I do talk to a handsome young man named Adam though, who, when I mention my dinner with Gil Cedillo, murmurs knowingly, "One Bill Gil."

"One Bill Gil"? He *has* had other bills besides the illegal alien driver's licenses, you know. For instance? A bill that would keep the fuzz from impounding the cars of people whose only crime is that they don't have licenses! "One Bill Gil"? That smarts.

Jennifer never does call, that dirty bitch.

And it's back to Chops. This is when lovely Tammy, the bartendrix, tells me that (a) she went to high school in Paducah, Kentucky, with Angels center fielder Steve Finley, and (b) the governor had been in here Monday night. At the same time I was.

Then the guy next to me, joining in the conversation, asks if I'd seen the governor's announcement that day.

"The governor made an announcement?" I ask.

Yes, he's going to fully fund Proposition 42, the law that says the gasoline tax must go to transportation projects. It was passed overwhelmingly in 2002, but first Gray Davis suspended it, grabbing $868 million (fiscal emergency) and then Schwarzenegger suspended it, diverting its $1.2 billion to other programs (fiscal emergency). So let's see what Schwarzenegger said this fine day: "The people voted to have [gas] tax money used for transportation. But the politicians, of course, had other ideas. They raided transportation funds to cover the deficits and their reckless spending. And our roads and infrastructure have suffered."

Yes. "The politicians." You tired? I'm tired.

My new friend pulls out a binder with all the relevant facts of the announcement Schwarzenegger had made at the League of California Cities luncheon.

"The governor was at the League of California Cities luncheon?" I ask.

I knew there was something I'd forgotten to do: like maybe ask the governor's office for his schedule.

I'm so fucking fired.

On the bright side: maybe they wouldn't have given it to me without a credential anyway! I'm pretty sure that's what I'll tell my boss.

I'm done with this town. My body is bloated from the vodka and ravaged by the waistband of my chic business attire of mismatched separates. Following a fruitless stint at the Hyatt, where the governor makes his home (I've tried but not succeeded to hang out long enough to let him get back from Fresno, as I'm falling into my drink), I'm back at the hotel, naked, in bed, when Lege staffer Juan calls. He wants me to get my ass dressed and come to Simon's, the Chinese restaurant of choice for politicos (well, after no. 1, Frank Fat's). He's hanging out with a bunch of staffers from Van Tran's office (R–Garden Grove). I don't *want* to go to Simon's!

I go to Simon's.

There, I listen, in totally over my head, as the staffers discuss the good old days of some San Diego race. I couldn't begin to guess what they're talking about. But eventually the talk turns to gun control. I know about gun control!

I confuse the Second Amendment with the Fourth. What the hell is the Fourth anyway? Unreasonable search and seizure? In that case, what's the Third? It's 1 a.m., and we start calling everyone we know to find out. Unfortunately, there are no libertarians nearby with their handy pocket Constitutions.

Still, I am a laughing stock. That very afternoon, when I'd run into former Assemblyman Tony Strickland at Chops, and he'd told me he's now the prez of the California chapter of Club for Growth? Yeah, then I'd been able to quote back to him some of national Club for Growth head Grover Norquist's greatest hits, like when he said that it was cool for the Republicans that more of the Greatest Generation was dying off each day, because they were all socialists who'd demanded the New Deal. Now, in addition to having called the governor's race for Tom McClintock, I don't even know the Second fucking Amendment, and the staffers have handed me my ass like the puppy owners handed Schwarzenegger his, when he tried to reduce the kill time at the state's pounds.

Shit. They'll probably think I'm some bimbo *broadcast* journalist or something. I'm mortified, appalled and humiliated.

I'm humiliated like Richard Riordan on Jay Leno's soundstage. I'm humiliated like Schwarzenegger's erstwhile friend, the one whose wife he publicly banged. I'm humiliated like any number of women held down and molested on rowdy movie sets—or even the British talkshow host he manhandled.

I'm still not bothering to put allegedly.

Sue me.

(And I still find that to be particularly well-put.)

I'm humiliated, and I'm out of there.

I should have gone to Fresno.

The Girl Who Peed Herself

Tuesday, March 7, 2000. 9:15 p.m.: We enter the Sutton Place Hotel in—natch—Newport Beach, to partay at the state's Republican election-night headquarters. We are immediately faced with a small sign reading "Media," beyond which (we deduce) lie sandwiches. We make a sandwich from the depleted deli trays, while the blonde in charge eyes us to ascertain that we are indeed working press. We're not sure if it's the leather pants or the slutty pigtails in charming lavender bows that make her suspicious, but we graciously reassure her and sail out of the room, sandwich held high.

9:19 p.m.: We travel several feet to the ballroom, from which a stampede emanates. The why is no mystery: a stageful of peppy urchins are "Celebrating America" in the most nasal manner. Their screeches are almost identical to those we hear outside our house when the entire neighborhood congregates to play World Wrestling Federation in our yard, at which point we have to scream out the window like a crack mom that if we hear one more kid yelling, we're gonna loose the rottweilers. USA! USA! Jazz hands, everybody!

9:26 p.m.: The lovable scamps have moved on to "Anchors Aweigh." We do a little soft-shoe.

9:27 p.m.: The risers in the back of the ballroom are crowded with news cameras, while the only people left seem to be clean-cut young reporters. They look ferociously bored. We mill about, trying to get on as many newscasts as possible. Did you see us? We grab a beer and balance it beneath our notebook as we write. We're good at that.

9:34 p.m.: The cherubs are chirping a rendition of Woody Guthrie's hippie-folkie love anthem "This Land Is Your Land." You recall, we're sure, that lots of groovy hippie folks advocate changing our national anthem from the bomb-and-rocket-filled "Star-Spangled Banner" to the fuzzy-wuzzy, graciously inclusive sing-along of Guthrie's biggest hit. Make love, not war! The kids are here to turn it into a jingoistic challenge to liberals. They shake pompons. Rah!

9:45 p.m.: A Bush supporter and a McCain supporter wave signs halfheartedly at each other, no doubt hamming it up for the cameras. The room is almost empty.

9:50 p.m.: Surfin' Congressman Dana Rohrabacher has taken the stage to ramble about the Strategic Defense Initiative. But don't take his word for it! Take the word of former Doobie Brother and Steely Dan lead guitarist Skunk Baxter! The ponytailed, beret-wearin' Republican is apparently some kind of big expert. Fucking ponytailed motherfucker. Dana returns to whip the crowd into a *Rollerball* blood lust. "Do we live in the best city? Do we live in the best state? Do we live in the best country in the whole world?" Dana entreats, and the crowd goes nuts and starts gnashing and foaming and tearing the heads off live chickens. Now this is more like it! Dana disappears behind a curtain.

9:57 p.m.: We spot a hipster punk rock girl, with dyed black hair and Buddy Holly glasses, wearing a No on Knight (the referendum that would proactively outlaw gay marriage in the state) sticker and waving a Bush sign. Her name is Natalie, and she is a senior at Newport Harbor High School. She gives us a No on Knight sticker because we were, until now, fitting in a little too well. You know, we love the gays. We do. (Although we hear from some of our girl-power friends that the ladies are falling off the lesbian tree left and right. We say love is where you find it, even if that's with someone of the opposite sex.) And it wasn't that long ago that California banned interracial marriage.

10:01 p.m.: *The YAFers attack!* We've been dreading it and, for just this purpose, we have corralled Jim the Futon Magnate (and former US Marine) into attending with us—for protection. He smoothly pushes us out of the elevator in which we've been cornered, and as the YAFers (Young Americans for Freedom) clamor and bitch, he shoves us into another elevator just before its doors close. Nice moves, Jim the Futon Magnate!

10:04 p.m.: Yup, the YAFers are waiting for us in Jim Righeimer's hospitality suite. Surprisingly, the dirty tricksters—and so proud of it—are warm and gracious and just want to be loved. Is that so wrong? Former state chairman Brian Park, perhaps looking for just a little more notoriety, offers to escort us about the hotel. Too bad he's such an evil young man. Righeimer is a terrific guy except he carries the far Right's water (he was responsible for Proposition 226, the Demonization of Teachers Act, two years ago; his strategy became so popular that even the "Center" guy on NPR's *Left, Right and Center* questioned whether then-gubernatorial candidate Gray Davis wasn't a little too cozy with teachers. They're teachers! TEACHERS!). Still, we adore Righeimer and his lovely, sweet supermodel wife, Lene. But Righeimer is losing badly in his campaign to replace termed-out Scott Baugh in the state Assembly. The victorious Tom Harman sent out a zippy four-page mailer calling Righeimer a deadbeat and outlining (with legal citations) several lawsuits and liens against him. It's no secret that he declared bankruptcy before the economy magically resuscitated itself; the mailer made him look like a big, fat creep. Come to think of it, it's very YAF—like their recent mailer accusing another candidate of poisoning dogs. We grab a beer from the bathtub.

10:14 p.m.: Security calls. An irate neighbor wants the folks at Righeimer's to keep it down. Righeimer can't get no respect. We grab another beer from the bathtub.

10:30-ish: Park walks us through the ground-floor presidential suites. Bush has a double suite, and McCain's is pathetically empty. A crazy Chinaman (that's really the only possible description) in national costume starts to shriek. We help ourselves to a beer and get gone.

10:40 p.m.: We meet the elusive Mrs Rohrabacher, Rhonda Carmony. She is a small, bright-eyed brunette with little make-up and a hell of a handshake. She's probably a terror in the arm-wrestling arena.

10:45 p.m.: A YAFer sexually harasses us. We begin yelling. It will be some time before we stop.

10:55 p.m.: A libertarian klatch, as *The Orange County Register*'s Alan Bock holds court with some YAFers; the *Times Orange County*'s Peter Warren, who won a coveted Orange County Press Club award for his exposé of hundreds of suspicious votes in the original Bob Dornan/Loretta Sanchez contest (large groups of people all registered at the same address; they of course turned out to be such deviants as nuns and Marines), looks dashing in a gray suit and bow tie.

11:20 p.m.: We save *Weekly* reporter R. Scott Moxley from the awful little man who has cornered him and is talking about how Senate candidate Tom Campbell is so Friedmanesque, at which point our incredibly cultured photographer, Jack Gould, inquires, "Milton Friedman? The father of supply-side economics?"

"No, he wasn't!" the little man shouts.

"Didn't the Reagan revolutionaries credit him with being the father of supply-side economics?" Jack persists.

"No!" screams the awful little man.

We exclaim, "Boys! We have to go to that thing now. You know. *That thing.* That we have to *go* to." Once again, we have saved the day.

12:08 a.m.: We have begun stalking reporters. The *Times'* Warren won't let Kate Dornan, pretty daughter of Bob, hug him. He reluctantly lets her shake his hand. The *Register's* handsome Martin Wisckol is interviewing someone important named Dick. We sit right down and introduce ourself. May we call him Dick? We may.

12:12 a.m.: Although our mind feels clear, we are losing our motor skills.

12:35 a.m.: Our notes become indecipherable: "Will the elonageadly go down?" We are trying to sober up, but it's difficult because we are still drinking.

1:10 a.m.: A girl in white stretchy capri pants saunters into the lobby. The assorted YAFers, state senators and drunken reporters go simultaneously quiet. She has peed her britches. There is no mistaking the drench pattern, from crotch almost to knees, down the inner thighs. She has not sat in something; she has definitely peed herself, and she does not even tie a sweater around her waist or walk knock-kneed to try to minimize the visible wet area. No. She struts, hips like weapons. We are all impressed.

real women wear black?

The referees were pretty good—for scabs. We've all seen regular referees do a lot worse, anyway. But I was going to have to keep my attendance at the Oakland Raiders/Green Bay Packers game on the down-low until I could figure out my rationalization—the regular officials having been locked out by the NFL. On Labor Day weekend!

We'd been looking forward to the game for months. We had tickets. We had plane tickets. And it was my boyfriend-type-person Bob's birthday, and he was as happy as Huntington Beach City Councilman Dave Garofalo in a pile of bribes about seeing Packer god Brett Favre throw, and on and on. But those slim reasons would be about as useful as Supervisor Jim Silva when Commie Mom found out we were crossing the line. I just wasn't going to tell her.

But Bob is an idiot. We were on our way to the game, and I was chatting on the phone with Emma Goldman herself when Bob said sweetly, "Let me talk to your mom!" Chuckling, he asked her if she knew her daughter was crossing a picket line to see scab referees officiate. On Labor Day weekend! Somehow he thought that would be funny—probably because he's a big Republican muckety-muck, and organized labor is hilarious to them. The mascara running down my face as I morphed instantly into Bette Davis as Baby Jane while my mother tersely reminded me that I was a grape-eating, Vons-shopping, big-Republican-muckety-muck-dating hypocrite probably clued him in. (In my defense, I didn't buy grapes for months even after the twenty-year boycott ended. And there never was a boycott against Vons. But according to my mother, serious people don't care if a boycott "ends" or "doesn't exist." She's tough.)

I wasn't going into it lightly; had there been an actual picket line, Bob would have been sitting in his Mark Chmura jersey (he's the Packer with a predilection for baby sitters) all by himself, though that's a matter of aesthetics more than principle probably. And I checked into the refs' demands. The NFL was offering a 50 percent raise. Referees work five months per year, about ten hours per week (and that's if they travel). And for that, a rookie official is already making 42 large. The NFL was offering 62 (again, for a rookie), to which the refs—all of whom in their regular lives are corporate bankers, VPs and commercial pilots—had turned up their noses like it was fruited Spam. And that pissed me off. I had tickets to see Rich Gannon, and these guys were gonna hold me hostage because they wanted $95,000 per year their first year out of the gate? For five months' work? On weekends? Do I make $95,000 per year? (Not including the value of the drinks I cadge?) Do you? Did the refs in question deny themselves grapes even once? What would Carlo Tresca say?

Nobody at Oakland's Network Associates Coliseum ("Meet me at the Net!") really seemed to care: the International Brotherhood of Electrical Workers marquee still shone next to the scoreboard; the Raiderettes still pranced. And the crowds still shook to the PA system's dirty, dirty rock & roll music— AC/DC, Motley Crue and more AC/DC—while Gannon and my new boy, Marques Tuiasosopo out of University of Washington, creamed the Packers 24–13. Even Bobby Hoying, the second-string quarterback whom I may never forgive for his disastrous showing in last year's playoffs after The Cannon got laid out, didn't suck entirely, though he still hasn't seemed to realize you're supposed to throw the ball *to* someone; it doesn't count if you just throw it into the end zone by itself. It was a game filled with loud, happy drunks eating plates of garlic fries and handing one another joints, the kind of bread and circus with which Rome used to pacify its hordes. But men and women who labor strong all through the week, even those whose greatest on-the-job risk is carpal tunnel syndrome, *need* bread and circuses. There must be some fun to look forward to on our weekends—weekends, by the way, that exist thanks to the Wobblies and the socialists and the anarcho-syndicalists.

There are no heroes here. The union is acting foolishly, the NFL is acting far worse, and I am in the strange position of not having the moral high ground from which to talk.

The sheer bad taste of a lockout on Labor Day weekend nullifies the natural advantage the NFL would have had by pointing out to the real working men— the Latino guys who were hammering outside my window at 7 on Labor Day morning for $5 per hour, for instance—how little they have in common with these refs, who most likely don't know their maids' names. And despite the silliness of the refs' demands, it was the NFL that broke off negotiations and locked out the officials, a fact I very conveniently didn't differentiate in my huff over the referees' tax bracket. My boss wants me to point out how merrily communists stab one another in the back as a way to assuage my own sins. Forget Trotsky versus Stalin; here in our own country, we had Big Bill Haywood and the Wobblies refusing to pony up support for Tresca and the Colorado miners. Even the anarchists refused to support their own Sacco and Vanzetti, letting the state have its sorry way with them to clear a few robberies. But while it's a fun exercise, it's as loudly diversionary (and even almost as intellectually dishonest) as the Republicans rioting and rattling on the windows outside the Miami-Dade counting rooms that led the Miami-Dade canvassing board— shockingly—to discontinue its vote count in January. But though I'm enduring the odd experience of feeling "guilt," I still can't spare a tear for the poor referees. My tears are already taken.

rushed

The boss seemed big on me going to the Rush Limbaugh Fan Club meeting at the Laguna Something Holiday Inn—Woods? Niguel? Hills? Is there a difference? Do you live there? If so, why? So I arose at the ridiculous time of 7:56 a.m. Saturday to leave the house at 8.00. I had been out with sweet Dana the night before, visiting pretty Haley and her mojitos at Avalon. Then we'd gone to the Little Knight to sober up, which was just foolish, now that I think about it. Seven fifty-six was looking as ugly as the Mount St Helen's sky outside. (You know what I say: the fires are clearly Bill Clinton's fault!)

I didn't want to go, and anyway, it wasn't like the Rush Limbaugh nuts were gonna let me in.

"I can tell my boss the Rush Limbaugh nuts wouldn't let me in," I told my boyfriend.

"No," my boyfriend said—before giving me a mumbled lecture about "work" and my "job."

Stupid boyfriend.

I got to the Laguna Something Holiday Inn perfectly punctually for the 8:30 breakfast and forked over fifteen clams as well as $7.50 for a fan club membership. I just thought it was so swell of them to offer—me, a member? Well, bless your heart!—plus I can never say no to anyone selling strawberries or magazines or memberships in right-wing nut-job fan clubs. I am what used-car salesmen call a *grape*.

"So how did you hear about us?" the kindly folks at the sign-up table asked.

"My editor at the *OC Weekly* wanted me to cover it," I said, my Tourette's-like honesty blowing my undercover status pretty quickly. Here's a dramatization of me as an undercover cop:

Perp: *You're not a cop, are you?*

Me: *Yes. Yes, I'm afraid so. I am a cop. Yes.*

Two minutes later, I was seated at a table for eight when the suave guy next to me offered, "There's a petition in the back to repeal the illegal alien driver's license bill."

I took a breath. "Actually, I'm a big liberal," I said. "I think the illegal alien driver's licenses are terrific."

Here's a dramatization of me undercover at a Klan rally:

Skinhead: Kill the Jews!

Me: No! Don't kill the Jews!

Skinhead: What are you, a Jew?

Me: Yes. Yes, I'm afraid I am a Jew. Yep. Big Jew, right here. I'm a Jew. That's me. I'm also a communist. Please don't kill me. Damn it!

After I outed myself, kindly old Phyllis changed the subject to the neutral one of her recent travels in lovely Vermont. I managed to hold my tongue about Bernie Sanders, Vermont's socialist congressman—not to mention those commies Ben and Jerry—and instead countered with tales of my own recent travels to Hawaii, where we went to Punchbowl Cemetery to visit my grandfather, who was a second lieutenant in World War II. See how subtly I establish my patriot cred? I am nothing if not subtle. On my other side, a man who seemed to be suffering from post-traumatic stress syndrome from a more recent war talked to himself. "What's that thing where the Japanese stayed in the planes?" he grunted.

"Kamikazes?" the others at the table offered quietly.

"Kamikaze," he said. "Okinawa's where the kamikazes are." And then he laughed with himself as he made plane-crashing-into-the-table motions. "Kamikaze," he said again.

The fans of our radio talkshow host began their meeting with lots of news and notices, like one about conservative website NewsMax offering a way to protest CBS's upcoming "hit piece" on Ronald Reagan. "Apparently the producers are two gay guys who hate Reagan," said the guy running the meeting, who was also kindly. Then Lorraine gave the invocation, which was much sweeter and more Christian than Jo Ellen Allen's had been at the OC Republican Election Night party (and where Jo Ellen called for Gray Davis' days to "be few"). If you would like to attend the Rush Limbaugh Fan Club's Christmas Dinner, it will be held in conjunction with the Leisure World Republican Club's on December 22 and will feature a "prime filet mignon and, you know, the usual fish." By which Lorraine did not mean Representative Chris Cox. He comes separate.

By the time county Supervisor Bill Campbell came up to talk about the new voting machines, I was bored stiff—but sweetly. (Really, the Rush Limbaugh nuts were incredibly welcoming, for which I applaud them.) Campbell talked about the difference between his service in the Assembly and his current service on the board, and then he gave a terrific rationale about why he and his fellow electeds avoid the woes of term-limit unemployment by job-swapping all up and down the ballot—he trained for public service on the public dime his first term, he said, and didn't know what he was doing until after; shouldn't he give the community the benefits of his publicly financed job training? Well rationalized indeed, Bill! Then he enthused on his work with Chris Cox, trying to get the police "cross deputized" so they can arrest illegal aliens for being illegal. "Great!" murmured the crowd. "Mmhmm!"

"That hasn't been challenged by the ACLU and the Nativo Lopez crowd?" someone shouted from the audience. The Rush crowd is an irrepressible lot! Not at all, replied Campbell. Seems Sheriff Mike Carona has a task force set to meet and explain to those same folks why it protects them from the browner hordes. The Rush Club's publicity intern, a pleasant and pretty young woman from Nigeria, spoke up in a melodious voice, wanting folks to know there are legal immigrants, too. The oldsters fell all over themselves reassuring her she's swell. They all like her! Then Campbell informed us there's new polling showing that the people in Iraq are not nearly as unhappy as the press claims. Tell it to Donald Rumsfeld, Bill. I seem to remember a leaked memo on the subject. As if all that weren't enough, Campbell told of his dinner with Justice Clarence Thomas. "What a marvelous man!" Campbell enthused. "He's raising his grand-nephew because the grand-nephew's father got in trouble and, you know, is in jail."

Say, you know who will never see a jail cell? Rush Limbaugh!

Just when I thought affable, reasonable-seeming businessman Bill Campbell (he's a former Taco Bell franchisee) couldn't get any red-meatier, he brought up Supreme Court Justice Antonin Scalia. "A heckler—who wanted 'under God' out of the Pledge of Allegiance—popped off in such a provocative way that Scalia said, 'What's wrong with "under God"?' and had to *recuse himself!*" Campbell is clearly outraged by the wily heckler's perfidy, but isn't Scalia supposed to be the Supreme Court's resident evil genius? How's he getting bested by some godless heckler? D'oh!

An old lady cited *The Orange County Register*'s Gordon Dillow—who is not the paper's resident evil genius (that's Alan Bock!), but is the paper's resident crotchety old coot. "In Gordon Dillow's column the other day," she kvetched—or would have if WASPs could—"he said it was about time to require IDs to vote."

Bill Campbell took it and ran. "The Democrats don't want us to," he said, very, very piously. "They say it's because it discourages people from voting, but I think it's because it discourages voter fraud."

Well, you smug, slanderous bastard.

After Campbell's presentation of the new voting machines and his right-wing bona fides, I spoke with Campbell's guy, Mark Denny. "Everyone I've spoken to is worried about the fact that there's no paper print-out with the computer voting," I told him. "Would it be possible to add that?"

"Sure," he said. "It's just a matter of adding some software."

So why didn't they?

"The Secretary of State didn't require it," he said.

"But he's a Democrat, so he clearly wants more *voter fraud*," I reminded him. Denny put up his hands.

"*I* didn't say that!" he murmured.

No, but your boss just did.

In the two hours I was there, a lot was said about Reagan, Scalia, Thomas, Todd Spitzer, Gordon Dillow and the American Enterprise Institute, but little was said about Our Hero, Rush Limbaugh. Not one word was spoken about Rush's recent disgrace—about his crackhead-crazy Oxycontin-popping that gives new meaning to the name "Rush"—or about Limbaugh's statement on the ESPN sports channel that Donovan McNabb isn't worthy of the Eagles uniform and remains a quarterback only because he's black and, therefore, a kind of pet project of the National Football League, a gift to the liberal media, but withal a scourge on American culture.

About the drugs, the Dittoheads said nothing. About McNabb—whose name the Rushies could not bring themselves to utter—one man said sadly, defensively, "It's been proven that he is overrated, which is all Rush was trying to say."

No, that wasn't all he was trying to say. As *Saturday Night Live*'s Tina Fey put it, Rush is the one guy who "has the guts to say what the liberal media doesn't want you to know: black people are not good at sports."

Since my new friends at the Rush fan club had too much class to try to excuse Rush's serious breach of etiquette in becoming a big, embarrassing, drug-addled loser, I had to go to my girl Annie Coulter to make some sense of it for me. Yes, here it is: Rush's addiction is Bill Clinton's fault, and by the way, did you know Ted Kennedy killed Mary Jo Kopechne?

But I won the raffle! How exciting is that? Since I couldn't stomach actually taking home *The Way Things Ought to Be*, I chose instead the book *And the World Came This Way: Jesse Helms' Contribution to Freedom*. I think me and the Rush Limbaugh Fan Club will get along just swell. We have to, since I'm its newest member. See you at the Christmas Dinner!

a mob of one

We were outside, between the pool, the keg and the fire pit, when one of my guests said to another, "I can't wait for your generation to fucking die!" He repeated himself in case the man to whom he was speaking hadn't picked up on his vehemence. "I cannot fucking wait!"

And to top it all off, the man was speaking thusly to his father-in-law.

I've had some pretty bitchen parties in my day, but this baby shower I was throwing was smokin'.

We were talking, of course, about Social Security—all the kids are doing it these days! The old guy is a libertarian asshole who doesn't believe in Social Security, giving poor people government cheese or immigration (he had some choice words about it in front of his own silent Mexican wife and also in front of the immigrant nurse who cares for our friend with MS). His son-in-law is in his mid-thirties, from Europe (I smell a socialist!) and really pissed off.

Can't our antipodal generations take a cue from alleged gropers Lindsay Lohan (who can vote now!) and the fifty-year-old Bruce Willis? Eh, probably not. Stupid, ugly old people.

Frankly—and for a change—I was pissed off, too. Did you know that aside from all the old folks (rescued from cat food since 1938) and the people with MS (who get disability checks), there are 275,000 children in California who receive survivors' benefits because their parents died? And did you know that my small buttercup of a son is one of them because he lost his first mommy when he was a baby? It was terribly careless of him, I'm sure.

I earn almost exactly California's median income—I'm livin' large, suckas! And yet, without my son's Social Security, there's no possible way (short of moving to Palmdale) we could live in a nice home with a backyard, where my boy gets a dog. (And she's a good dog! Oh, yes, she is!) We would live in the ghetto like we used to, where the neighbors liked to have gun fun in the front— and sometimes, there were murders!

But now I'm ashamed. Look how *entitled* I am, hissing and scratching for that government handout that my son's first mom paid into the system! I remember reading letters to Dear Abby about women who were witnessed at the grocery store buying fresh strawberries with food stamps. God, I'm so selfish! Selfish, selfish, selfish!

Really, I should be more poor.

I've been reading everything possible on Social Security, including wonkfests like Josh Marshall's Talking Points Memo, which is so very inside baseball it should be fashioned from cork. Not only that, but last week, I had a fifty-minute conversation about OC's troubled public pension fund that was freaking *enthralling*.

So, really, my point is I enjoy boring things.

And that's why I went to the Social Security Town Hall meeting at the Teamsters Local 952 in Orange on Saturday morning, with lots of oldsters, someone's teenage son and his four buddies, several black folk, and some people in faux-satin union windbreakers.

Now, how do I explain to you the Bush administration's plan for Social Security without putting you into your soup? To recap it simply: when a group (USA Next) funded by the guys behind the Swift Boat Vets goes after the American Association of Retired Peoples (AARP) by claiming AARP is for gay marriage and against The Troops™, you can pretty much figure they don't have a lot of positive points on which they can rely. And when the most explicit explanation the Bush administration puts forth for the Social Security plan is a memo from Grand Old Party pollster Frank Luntz to GOP types claiming that in order to win, facts and figures should be avoided (since they contradict the administration's claims), you can be pretty sure that, like the old Suicidal Tendencies chestnut, your best interests are not what they have in mind.

In the shortest, least-dull paragraph I possibly can: Baby Boomers have been putting money into the Social Security trust fund; in forty or fifty years, that cushion of money will run out, and the incoming monies will pay only 80 percent of promised Social Security benefits. Bush's plan: divert a percentage of payroll taxes into private accounts to be invested in the stock market. If your stocks do well, you pay back the government for any benefits it "gave" you, and if there's anything left over, you buy yourself an annuity that gives you the poverty rate for the rest of your miserable old life. If your stocks fail (which, as Enron knows, *never happens*), there *is no guaranteed benefit*. No annuity, not even at the poverty rate.

Oh, yeah, and the transition to this new system is gonna cost $2 trillion.

Oh, yeah, again: they admit it does nothing to solve the "crisis."

Oh, yeah, a third time. Survivors' benefits? Those won't be necessary, but thanks.

In order to dismantle the nasty, socialist old Social Security, Bush's people have been triangulating *beautifully*: old vs young (done and *done!*), black vs white (last week, the president said his critics were racists who don't believe blacks are smart enough to invest their own money), and women vs men (some Republicans have suggested giving women smaller benefits than men because we live longer, and Rush Limbaugh helpfully explained that we live longer because our lives are so easy; selfish, easy-living old me!). But as hard as the Republicans are working (because being president is hard work!), the people just refuse to buy! The president's approval rating on the subject is a terrible 36 percent.

And that's why it was so nice to go to that god-durned ol' Town Hall meeting. Men, women, blacks, whites, teens (under duress), and lots and lots of old folks gathered together with state Senator Joe Dunn and Congresswoman Loretta Sanchez and some really shitty coffee to be outraged, insulted and pissed off as one.

Loretta's never been one of my favorite people—and she probably returns the favor—but on this morning, in her soft pink suit, as she stood onstage and asked—shrieked—of our Dear Leader, "Is he *insane?*" I felt some love in my shriveled old heart. She explained the president's plan and its problems, she threw out some of Luntz's fearful facts and figures (before Social Security, fully two-thirds of seniors lived under the poverty line while today just 16 percent do, and as for the wonders of the stock market, last year Republican Senator Bill Frist himself evaporated half a million in campaign funds that had wisely been invested in it), and she gave us some insight into Washington maneuvers. "What are we gonna do," she asked, "put seven-year-olds to work? The Republicans have been saying—even a few Democrats have said to me personally—'We can get rid of survivors' benefits; just make it a retirement program.'" Her voice reaching a level that hitherto only dogs could hear, she screeched, "What do we do with these people?"

It was nice to see Loretta with her dander up. Fight for your right to fight!

If you're my age—an adorably spring-chickenish thirty-two—you've been told by the Republicans for years that Social Security won't be there when you're old and miserable and smell like mothballs.

They were lying, and we bought it, and now we want "personal" accounts* like our 401(k)'s. You know what we have now that's like our 401(k)'s?

Our 401(k)'s.

Franklin Delano Roosevelt, in that dashing way of his (and probably with that cigarette clamped 'tween his teeth), called for three parts to our retirements: defined Social Security benefits to provide a minimum level on which to rely; personal savings like the 401(k)'s; and pensions. None of us gets a pension anymore except for public employees, and Schwarzenegger's on a mission to kill those. Our 401(k)'s could tank any time—ask the nice people who lost their money during the 2001 "correction." And folks now are saying that the Dems can't just be obstructionists; we can't just be the Party of No.

Yes! We can!

No!

It's not up to us to figure out an acceptable way to dismantle Social Security just because the Bushes still call FDR "that man."

Some people think Bush's plan is a $2 trillion sop to Wall Street. He's never been against a back-scratch, but more, it's a fundamental Calvinist trope: Bush and his family are wealthy because they're good. (You know, except for Neil.)

And Social Security is socialism they were against from the beginning. Now, as their trusted ideologue Grover Norquist says, it's the first time in sixty years they've had all their branches of gubmint sewn up, and for the first time, they can pay those New Dealies back. I'd say it's sick, but you know I don't like to preach.

Except for this: It's not up to us to provide their cover. And it fo' sho isn't up to us to have my mom live with me when she's ancient and even crotchetier than she is now.

Matlock!

Let the old folks have their independence. Pay your stupid payroll taxes, and the kids will pay theirs when you're on the dime.** Don't let yourself get divided with who's getting more because those assholes want to make sure most of us don't get *any.* And while we're at it, don't begrudge welfare moms some fucking strawberries once in a while, you mean old nasty coot.

As Dear Abby explains, it makes you look small.

* Calling these accounts "private" is biased, White House Press Secretary Scott McClellan says, because the president doesn't call them that anymore.
** It's how civilization's supposed to work, just ask John Locke!***
Unless you prefer your Hobbesian life: nasty, brutish and short.*
****Like Neil Bush!*****
*****But I don't like to preach.

The mommy party

I think we all know that I snit easily. Take just this morning (please!) and the snit I got into from someone (we'll call him "Tad") e-mailing me a nice note that ended with, "By the way, I love that you're a mommy." (Any use of proper punctuation is coincidental or has been added by me.) I replied, without being overly horrible about a grown man using the word "mommy"—since there was no need to get into What Exactly Was Wrong With Ronald Reagan this early in the game—"I'm not a mommy so much as a mom, since my son's eleven," and added a sentence or two about my parenting philosophy—trying to make my son more independent, etc.—when Tad answered back, "You'll always be a mommy; that's the gift you received when you had your son."

Okay, breathe.

Surely the guy was just trying to be nice. Am I an asshole? Was I reading *way* too much into it by seeing it as a man pompously correcting me—and infantilizing me with the cloying baby talk while he was at it—and determining for me my proper place in the world? That Tad, who's never met me, didn't listen to what I was saying, and had to spout homilies from *Chicken Soup for the Soul* to add insult to insult? He's gonna tell me what my "gifts" are? Him and his Dr Laura Virgin Mother Mommy Cult?

I know I'm a knee-jerk feminist, but am I insane in the bargain?

I told him (nicely, for me) why it had bugged me, but took the blame on myself for being overly bitchy and said I truly hoped he had a good day. He responded that I had issues and clearly needed counseling and said it was no wonder I don't have a boyfriend. Then he thanked me for showing him early how ugly I was on the inside.

Hey, motherfucker, where's your *Chicken Soup* now?

This was at least the third guy on Yahoo Personals who'd told me I had issues. I was starting to believe them.

And that's when I started thinking about Harriet Miers.

"Mom!" I said. "I think I have issues, and I'm going to end up a 62-year-old spinster like Harriet Miers, and then everyone will snicker about why I never got married!"

"She's a lesbian," my mom explained sunnily. Yes, the 1987 mullet of Bush's former legal counsel—and Supreme Court nominee—was a bad idea.

"Well, people are going to think *I'm* a lesbian!" I said. "Or they're going to say, 'What kind of person is *sixty-two* and never got married?' like it's so not normal! I don't think she's a lesbian! I think Nathan Hecht just never married her because he was running around with Priscilla Owen, and she waited for him all those years, and it's supposed to be *her* fault he never married her! 'Too busy with her career,' my ass!"

"I think you'll get married," my mom said. "I think he'll be ugly, and he'll probably have money because I think it's important to you that a real man be successful and able to take care of things, and he'll love you and adore you exactly the way you are instead of trying to make you into that stupid mommy shit. Look at your cousin Caroline at her wedding: she was sucking Gary's fingers! She looooves him! She was kissing his neck on the dance floor! And he paid a lot of money for that beautiful wedding so they could have exactly what they wanted and didn't have to ask anybody, because he looooves her, and she's not sweet and soft! And you were right about that Tad guy: he's a disgusting asshole!"

I love my mom.

So I got in another fight (I am my mother's daughter), this time with Max. "I'm a Marine," Max boomed, presumably in the sense that once a Marine, always a Marine, since he's Santa-fat and has eight inches of biker beard jutting out of his chin. Max and I were having a charming conversation on the Swallow's patio, where I'd gone in a snit to stalk some folks who'd done me wrong, which, as you know, is most of them.

A most delicious car chase had just ended blocks from the door, with all of us whooping at the TV each time we saw the perp pass another Laguna Niguel offramp. Somewhere close, he exited, flipped a bitch and leaped out of his car running. But he wasn't fast enough for SuperCop (clearly, no doughnuts), who caught up to the perp like he was taking a Sunday stroll and took him out with a lovely and effective flying tackle.

"Yay!" shouted we inside, and I went onto the patio to pass on the exciting car-chase news. That's when Max started in on the ACLU. Why? I don't know, because Max was very, very drunk, which I understand, but what I don't understand is why everyone's got a hard-on for the ACLU.

Max: Fuckin' ACLU!

Me: Hey, what's wrong with the ACLU? They defend everyone's rights, whether they agree with you or not! The Constitution is the most beautiful document in history, and they defend *everyone's* constitutional rights, whether you're a liberal or a right-winger or a Nazi! Even if you're a total asshole, they'll defend your rights.

Max: They're only about letting minorities do whatever they want! Take South Central!

Me: Okay! What about it?

Max: All the criminals in South Central are black or Latino!

Me: Well . . . everyone in South Central is black or Latino, so, yes!

Max: If they arrest a white guy in South Central and give him special privileges because he's white, then they get in trouble.

Me: [. . .]

Max: I have a lot of friends who are black or Latino! [Begins a long tale of his Latino gunner, because he is very, very drunk.]

Me: Yes, you're a Marine. I totally believe that you have a lot of black and Latino friends. So . . . what's your point?

Max: My point is . . . I'm not racist!

And that's when I started thinking about Harriet Miers again. We're exactly alike, except that she's old and rough-looking and a fundamentalist Christian and George W. Bush's "work wife," and I'm young and pretty and have never had a mullet and don't ever remember anyone's birthday. Also, I have taken constitutional law.

Marbury vs Madison! Dred Scott! Griswold! Lemon vs Kurtzman!

Three prongs!

What the hell *is* everybody's problem with fighting for our constitutional rights and due processes? Why did the Purdue Youth Opinion Polls of the 1950s and 1980s find that American kids think the Bill of Rights maybe doesn't include religious freedom if it's applied to non-Christians, and why were those kids so happy to let the fuzz in without a warrant so long as the fuzz were after blacks? Why is it up to, like, me and New York Democratic Senator Chuck Schumer to give a fuck? Why the constant hate for the ACLU, which just opened up its first OC office, and I forgot to send a muffin basket? And what do we do about Harriet?

I don't know, frankly. The president did manage to confuse me but good. Nevada Democrat Harry Reid's for her? The far Right's losing its shit—and, without a drop of irony, is saying she hasn't made her views clear enough, even though when we said that all of three weeks ago vis-à-vis John Roberts we were "obstructionist" "scoundrels" and "scallywags"? Is their short-term memory truly so shot? And can I have some of that?

My pal Jim Washburn sent me a Carl Sandburg poem this week. It goes a little-something like this:

"I AM the people—the mob—the crowd—the mass. Do you know that all the great work of the world is done through me? I am the workingman, the inventor, the maker of the world's food and clothes. I am the audience that witnesses history. The Napoleons come from me and the Lincolns. They die. And then I send forth more Napoleons and Lincolns.

"I am the seed ground. I am a prairie that will stand for much plowing. Terrible storms pass over me. I forget. The best of me is sucked out and wasted. I forget. Everything but Death comes to me and makes me work and give up what I have. And I forget.

"Sometimes I growl, shake myself and spatter a few red drops for history to remember. Then—I forget. When I, the People, learn to remember, when I, the People, use the lessons of yesterday and no longer forget who robbed me last year, who played me for a fool—then there will be no speaker in all the world say the name 'The People' with any fleck of a sneer in his voice or any far-off smile of derision. The mob—the crowd—the mass—will arrive then."

It's like Chicken Soup for Non-Assholes.

i scream, you scream

I've been feeling my inner raving lunatic coming on for months now—haven't you?—and I found the most delightful outlet for it just last Wednesday: sitting atop a banquette in a meeting room at a Coco's in Mission Viejo, I screamed at a bunch of ancient South County Democrats (and waved my arms around like Hitler) until each and every one of them rolled over to let me scratch his or her soft, padded underbelly. Who's your alpha male? I'm your alpha male!

And oh, how they loved it.

They thought it was hilarious when I explained to them that I had *thought* they were beautiful (despite the fact that they are terribly old), but I had changed my mind since all they wanted to do was ask my colleague Jim Washburn question after question—positively bathing themselves in Jim's profundities—while I sat there, pretty and petite, and hadn't even given my goddamn speech yet! That's right! They weren't so beautiful after all! Nor was I too pleased to be there!

"Why are you asking *him* all the questions?" I shrieked at them. "Is it because he's a man?!" Yes, I was PMSing, thank you, and I'm freaking happy to say so!

Let's see you try to menstruate, Washburn! Go ahead! I'll wait.

I told them, further, that they better try not to sound crazy when they're talking to their neighbors, because they do sound crazy and they damn well know it!

Really, I was terrific. Jim was good too.

"Please, Rebecca," said *les anciens*, rolling and snuffling in masochistic glee, "may we have some more?"

Then we had us some faith healings, and, as always, I closed with a little soft-shoe.

Except I also talked (yelled and berated, really) about a lot of other shit as well, and considering I was just a tiny bit drunk (*not my fault*, since I'd been to a very fancy art opening, where I was discreetly adored by very old and very famous artists, until just moments previous), I had just a masterful command of my facts, if not so much my syntax. FACT: The 44 US senators representing Blue states represent 9 million more "folks" than the 55 US senators representing Red states. So every time some asshole starts piously intoning about Senate Democrats obstructing the will of the people (although no one seems to be weeping hot salty tears for the will of the people who elected the Senate Democrats!), well, wouldn't it be nice if we could kill him?

Oooh, sorry. That's something Texas Republican Senator John Cornyn would say, and I apologize! I really do! See, calling for someone's death (I mean besides retired Baltimore Raven Anthony Siragusa, but I didn't so much call for his *imminent* death as for him to die "lonely and alone," presumably at some far-off, and therefore even more depressing since he'd then be *old*, date) is something even I would consider beyond the pale. Did Cornyn apologize for stating during the Schiavo feeding frenzy (get it?) that violence against judges was understandable? Not so much, to my knowledge. Did Karl Rove apologize for just last week accusing Democrats of committing treason? No, and he never the fuck will—and for all the people demanding that he apologize? Stop it! Your oversensitive pussy is showing!

Hey, did y'all hear this week when Republican Senator Rick "Man on Dog" Santorum said the Catholic Church molestation scandal epicentered in Boston because Boston was a center of liberalism? Dude, liberals are *totally* child molesters—just ask Scott Ritter, the UN weapons inspector whose report that said Iraq had no weapons of mass destruction was derided by folks in the administration who smeared him as—you guessed it!—a child molester.

We're batshit? No, *you're* batshit, you batshit motherfuckers!

To prove it, here's a post from FreeRepublic.com hypothesizing eloquently on who will replace Sandra Day O'Connor on the Supreme Court (for my money? It'll be Hitler!). And when Sandra Day O'Connor is considered the Civilized One by the Left, we're in for happy, happy pain time. Oh, so let's look at what the batshit say:

I dont think that Alberto Gonzalez will get nominated, because who wants to eat Chimineychangas every day, not me.

But Democrats lately have been apologizing for just anything they could find. Like Governor Schwarzenegger having to turn to other candidates' promises since he'd run out of his own to break, the Dems lately have taken to apologizing for other people's sins. And, really, I'm starting to get a wee bit pissed.

Illinois Senator Dick Durbin last month came in for a rash of shit because he said the way we were treating prisoners at Guantanamo was un-American. He compared it to some really bad dudes, like Pol Pot and—yes—Hitler, to show just how un-American it is to detain people without access to lawyers and—oh, yeah—hang some from wires and beat others until they were dead.

After a couple of weeks of Fox News and some unholy Democrats (proving just how "moderate" they could be by disavowing him the way the Dems denied Michael Moore and, while we're at it, Peter denied Christ) beating the holy hell out of Durbin for saying the H word when, damn it (and these were their true examples of the US's beneficence in the matter), we give them meals and they get to serve their detention in the tropics (although I believe John McCain's palatial suite in the Hanoi Hilton was tropical, too, no?), well, Durbin *apologized.*

But you know who never backs down? The South County Democrats know. Howard Dean, one-time presidential candidate and current head of the Democratic National Committee. Motherfucker never stands down, no matter how much faux angst is wept by pundits accusing him of being batshit and out of line. Oh, I'm sorry. Did Howard Dean say that the Republican Party is pretty much exclusively white and Christian? Well, tear my hair! Let's see: *What* got avoided on the news that week because Howard Dean said the Grand Old Party was white and Christian? (And by the way, I'd like to see what happened if you accused one of them of being a Mexican Jew.) Oh. Huh. Well, that same week, the *extremely* controversial Janice Rogers Brown got her ass into a lifetime seat on the DC Circuit Court of Appeals. The Senate voted for further Patriot Act police powers.

Nothing to see here, folks.

Oh, right: and people were starting to have to *work* to avoid the July 2002 Downing Street Memo, that observed that the Bush administration was "fixing" the intelligence in order to provide a pretext to invade Iraq.

Enter Howard Dean!

And so I told the sweetling old folks at the South County Dems meeting— and I'm telling your ass now—send the man money!

Send him $5, $20, $500, or some Monopoly money with a cheery little note. Or, you know, just go have a drink and scream at people on the way.

montezuma's revenge

The people who used to live at my boyfriend's trailer down in Quatro Casas (about three hours south of Ensenada, thirteen miles from the highway down a rutted dirt road, fifty yards from a cold, shitty ocean) had a rare kind of ambition for Baja. I know this because the *her* of the couple left behind a captain's log of her every visit. It was good reading: she'd be all, "This morning I went for a run up the mountain, then we surfed twice and had lobster for lunch. Then we poured cement for the new steps." And I would laugh and laugh!

Here's my captain's log, star date last weekend: "Day Three: today, I put on lip gloss. Mike said it looked very nice."

I really needed a vacation. I could tell because the thought of having to write sentences with words and nouns and adjectives and punctuation and interesting thoughts and some funny jokes too was starting to give me some kind of anxiety disorder that would require Paxil or pot, and I'm plumb out of Paxil.

Also, I was starting to have housewife fantasies. Being one or having one, didn't make me no nevermind.

And it was maybe the best vacation ever! Mike took me to a flea market to buy used sweatpants because I was cold, and he took pictures of me passed out in the fire, and he hit me with a stick, and he peed my name in the dirt. It was super-romantic!

And I didn't miss you fuckers even one little bit.

"But why did he hit you with a stick?" my editor wanted to know as I showed him pictures of my boyfriend in the shower, the qualms of personnel managers and my boyfriend's feelings be damned.

"Because he likes me!" I answered. "Duh!"

But apparently I can't take my eyes off you people for four fucking days without you storming in and wrecking the place. Four days! A personal day on either side of a weekend! That is not a lot to ask! And I come back to find out that in the exalted GOP tradition of naming David Duke to the Civil Rights Commission and Christopher Cox to chair the Securities and Exchange Commission, El Prez waited for the Senate to recess, and then, over its moans and keens and bitches, named John Bolton—the man Republican Senator George Voinovich called "the poster child of what someone in the diplomatic corps should not be"—our new ambassador to the UN. The UN, of course, is the august body nasty old Bolton's called for abolishing and at some of whose members he's probably thrown shoes.

That is not a euphemism.

And this is why we can't have nice things!

I'm still reeling from the Bolton news, and learning more about Supreme Court nominee John Roberts—a guy who seemed like the best we could hope for given Georgie's predilection for insane nominations—remember the OB-GYN who wouldn't prescribe birth control to sinners (I mean single girls) being named head of reproductive medicine at the FDA? (As Molly Ivins wrote that she'd been thinking, "Sounds like [Roberts]'s about as good as we can get. Quick, affirm him before they nominate Bork, Bolton or Pinochet.") Except . . . whoops! Roberts has argued that *Griswold v. Connecticut* was wrongly decided, and *Griswold*, as you no doubt already know, was the decision that said you couldn't prosecute married couples for using birth control, ushering in the very same constitutional right to privacy that gets Pennsylvania Senator Rick Santorum so very overheated and frothy and unleashing terms like "man-on-dog." (Santorum's new book also bemoans women not marrying and working outside the home. Find *me* a housewife, Rick Santorum! I'll keep her real nice!) Meanwhile, in Wisconsin, Republicans are passing bills forbidding state colleges from dispensing birth control to co-eds—but the boys can still get their love gloves. What's with the Right's hard-on for knocking me up? Now they're not gonna let me have the Pill? Try telling that to Loretta Lynn. Fuck me! Or, rather, don't.

So all that's going on, and your American president is spouting off about how, hey, why *not* have Intelligent Design taught alongside evolution, while his poor science adviser, John Marburger, has stated point-blank, "Evolution is the cornerstone of modern biology" and, "Intelligent Design is not a scientific theory." Christ, what a thankless job that must be.

And then there was a plane crash, and something was up with the Space Shuttle, and Nate's fucking dead—AGAIN!—and in four days, nineteen guys from the same Ohio battalion ate it in Iraq in separate incidents and then All the President's Men changed the name of the Global War on Terror to the Global Struggle Against Violent Extremism, which, though unwieldy, is actually a better philosophy as far as I'm concerned, but I'm pretty sure it wouldn't change anything as far as the rights of "enemy combatants in wartime" go, not that it matters since I got to see with my own eyes Bill O'Reilly loftily instructing John McCain on the effectiveness of torture. Torture? Like the films from Abu Ghraib that Republican Senator Lindsay Graham described with obvious pain as "video of rape and murder"? Hey, they get lemon chicken and rice pilaf! But then the president bitched that no one consulted *him* about the name change, and you kind of cringed because you figured, *Of course they didn't.*

So I take two personal days—*two*—and people in the office had to pick up all kinds of slack. My sweet Theo had to write Eight Days, and Patty had to do who knows what all, and Sherry Wine had to go get drunk. But the president, his work here done, goes on a five-week vacation to his ranch at Crawford—the forty-ninth of his presidency, for a total of just under 20 percent of his terms so far—and everybody tries to spin that he still *works* at his ranch (you know, like he was working in August and September 2001), so it's not like he's on vacation, and it's left to me to remind you that he doesn't even work at the White House: he takes two-hour breaks in the middle of each day, and as governor of Texas, he was known for playing computer Solitaire while being briefed on clemency petitions from those about to be executed. Oh, well. It's not like they *consult him* on shit.

What a fucking dick.

I need another vacation.

The Silly Season

"Mom," my small buttercup of a son said out of nowhere two weeks ago while we were in the car listening to Randi Rhodes, "I can't wait to meet Howard Dean!" Fuckin' right, you can't, son! That's why when Phil Bacerra, executive director of the Orange County Democratic Foundation, called to tell me with great sadness—and possibly trepidation—that Howard Dean's cocktail meet-and-greet in Santa Ana last Tuesday would be, by order of the Democratic National Committee, a press-free zone, well, old Phil got just the smallest little piece of my mind.

"Did you tell them?" I screeched. "Did you tell them I am not Tucker Carlson? Did you tell them my newspaper is really not the same as *The Orange County Register*? That we are, in fact, the Liberal Media? That we *like* Howard Dean and think he is fantastic and are in fact big fans of the Fifty State Strategy? Did you tell them that we even know what the Fifty State Strategy is? And that we are fans of it? And that we are not Tucker Carlson?"

Phil had told them. They still said no. And my boy—the only boy in history to tell his mama, "I can't wait to meet Howard Dean!"—was in fact not going to get to meet Howard Dean.

Well, calls were made and folks were browbeat, until one of them cut Solomon's baby in half. My boy and I could attend the reception as guests of the DNC, but it was to remain off the record. I explained that I no longer go off the record, having decided last year (in the wake of watching Angel Adam Kennedy get blown in a parking lot) that it was not my place to mediate truth for the masses. I explained that I am not Tucker Carlson. I explained that after all these years of making fun of local Dems for not doing anything exciting—

or anything at all—I would really like to be able to credit them with a fun, fantastic event starring the one-and-only Mr. Governor Dean.

And then, about twenty seconds later, faced with the prospect of not taking my boy to see Howard Dean, I went off the record.

It turns out it's *easy* trading ethics for access: maybe I'll make a mainstream reporter yet! But first, let me think of something *nice* to say about President Bush.

It was a lovely party, and the governor was warm and much more patient with the retail-politics meet-and-greet-every-damn-person-there than I would have expected, and he didn't say a single thing that even Tucker Carlson could have twisted into crazy-talk—and I saw Tucker Carlson practically wet his pants two weeks ago because Howard Dean said "Jewish." Tucker Carlson is such a douche.

It was a perfect mini-silly season all last week, with just six weeks to go till the all-important June primaries. Monday I'd seen Herr Schwarzenegger—and, rest assured, he saw parts of me—where I'd been cowed into silence by my complete inability to ever be rude, or at least to ever be rude in person. Monday night, having had a few hours to rue my cowardice, I took it out on former assemblyman Tony Strickland (now running for state controller against our much-loved Joe Dunn) by grilling him during the Q&A at a meeting of the Young Republicans at the Clubhouse. Tuesday was (Don't) Meet the Press with Governor Dean. Wednesday was Muldoon's for the Young Dems with Fightin' Rocky Delgadillo, taking on Jerry Brown in the race for attorney general. And on Saturday I went to a dinner party at the home of my friends Jon and Deb Webb, where an impromptu presidential straw poll for 2008 went two for Joe Biden, one for Russ Feingold (he's the liberalest!) and three for Al Gore, though one of Gore's votes originally went for Eugene V. Debs and only switched to Gore after her point had been made. So basically, it was really the best dinner party ever, after which I went home and there was Al Gore on *Saturday Night Live*, being all dreamy and wry, as a tear trickled down my cheek for the Anti-Hurricane Machines that might have been lo these past six years.

A delightful week! *Delightful*, I . . . I'm sorry, am I boring you? Would it make you feel better if I said I was drunk?

Now, what was Tony Strickland saying? It was a pretty good stump speech, actually, going something like, if I remember correctly, "Lie, lie, lie, lie, lie." The Q&A—oooh, oooh! Pick me!—started out well enough, with someone asking why all these economic "conservatives" want us mired in perpetual debt with the tax cutting and refusing to pay for what we consume. (Personally, *someone* blames John & Ken and their hard-on for the car-tax rebate, after which nobody could figure out why California is $37 billion in debt.) But it didn't get fun till we started talkin' Supply Side Economics—or "a rising tide lifts all yachts"— which Strickland, being an economic conservative, is *for*, and *someone* asked, "Yeah, how's that working out on the federal level?" because *someone* is *hilarious*, and then he left pretty quickly after that, and my friend Shawn Fago said sort of wistfully that he wished I hadn't come. Also, I led the flag salute. So Monday was super-fun!

Then came Tuesday, which you already didn't read about, and Wednesday night was the Young Dems' turn! So what rude thing did I ask LA city attorney Rocky Delgadillo, running for attorney general? I didn't! He was very handsome.

But someone sitting on the fringe of the event did have something rude to say, and if I told you it was a table full of blond bigots in the corner of Muldoon's, would you be even the slightest bit surprised? Delgadillo, who is in fact very handsome, was talking about the terrible dropout rates for minority kids and had just uttered the word "Latino" when the cunt in the corner stopped yammering loudly with her friends long enough to shriek, "Make 'em *legal*!" Delgadillo kept talking, perhaps figuring, "Orange County," while some of us glared and the rest tried really hard not to. When the chair of the Young Dems was thanked for the event and rose from that very same table, I decided I'd misunderstood. The blonde, who clearly was a friend of hers, must have been talking up amnesty! So why had she sounded like such a god-awful bitch?

Fariel, the lovely young chairperson, explained later she'd gone over to the table only to politely beg them to be quiet for just a few moments so people in the back could hear, and the entitled misses had responded nastily, "I thought you were about *free speech*! Why are you trying to *censor* us?" So that's why I'm never rude in person: because I'm not a filthy twat.

Being arnold schwarzenegger

"What is this place?" my small buttercup of a son asked me curiously as we pulled up to the gate.

"This is a gated community, son!" I explained. My son is eleven years old and apparently has never been inside one of Orange County's most beloved inventions. I am clearly doing *something* right.

We were there—at whichever amalgamation of the words *park, acres* and *estates* that particular gated community happened to comprise—for a Teachers for Westly event, mostly because it was a Tuesday evening, and on Tuesday evenings I help out at my paper. Any reason to get out of the office would have sufficed: I would have shown up if I'd been invited to a seminar on dental health or a gab-and-grab with the governor. Oh, who'm I kidding? *Especially* a gab-and-grab with the governor!

Steve Westly, for the 29,998,780 of you Californians who don't know, is our state controller. He is running for governor. He is a wee, small man, and he needs caps on his kind of shardy, ocher teeth, and he helped found eBay. I would be reminded of this rather quickly when one of the Democrats in attendance said jovially to my boy, "It's probably the first time you'll get to meet a real billionaire!" ("Only maybe half a billion," demurred one of the young Dem lawyers who'd organized the event.) Ah. This is how Democrats do it in the OC.

I would have dulled my horror with a quick shot, but I'm sober now so I just smiled, though painedly. How'm I supposed to teach my child proper class warfare with that kind of attitude? He's already a bit fancy, with his taste for caviar, love of *Riviera* parties and completely unironic desire to possess necklaces with his name in four-inch letters of solid gold. Also, he wants a McMansion—and now, probably, in a gated community! Thanks a lot, OC Dems!

And by the way, you have terrible hair!

It was a very nice party, with sandwiches and such. I'm a big fan of sandwiches. Steve Westly? Well, he's no state Treasurer Phil Angelides (who's wonky and adorable and is also running for governor), but I figured it was only fair to give him a listen, despite all the lawyers who kept nodding about how important it was to nominate a "pro-business" Democrat. You want a pro-business Democrat? I would remind you that we had one until quite recently. His name was Gray Davis, or, as I like to call him, Exhibit A.

There was a short lull where I had to actually talk to people, so I cornered Bill Hunt, who's running for sheriff against Ralph Martin (some guy from the LA sheriff's office) and Mike Carona (everyone's favorite sexy gladhander), and asked him excellent questions such as, "If the guys from OC Blog knew you were here, you'd be toast." Then I asked him, "You know, I hear good things about Ralph Martin!" Hunt tried to stump me with his answer to that one: "If you don't care that he doesn't know Orange County."

"He lives in Orange County!" I riposted.

"Well, if you consider Coto de Caza Orange County," riposted he back.

"Actually, it's probably the ne plus ultra Orange County, if you think about it," riposted I cubed. And it is. Perhaps my son will take me in when I'm old and living on Meow Mix and he's living the Caza life in his tract home fashioned from solid gold.

You know: with his name on it.

Then my son wanted to know if Hunt, who's much more attractive and less gangly in person than in his campaign pix, was married. My son is always trying to pimp me out, asking me leading questions like, "Did you think the parking lot attendant was handsome, Mom?" and "Do *you* think you look fat in your bathing suit?"

Westly ran into the room of about thirty bystanders, the better to showcase the Ed Grimley energy his consultants must have recommended, and began his education stump speech. He was reasonably progressive, for a pro-business

Democrat, and in certain cases very progressive, unapologetically taking positions for which John & Ken will doubtless flay him, probably about fourteen minutes from . . . *now.* Of course, with the crowd he stood before (on the stairs; like I said, he's kind of shrimpy), there was no reason to apologize for confirming to us that illegal alien kids who've grown up here and gone to high school here should pay in-state tuition at our state colleges—the current mangy, rabid lather of the California Coalition for Immigration Reform floozies. If he'd given any other answer than "AB-SO-LUTELY" to the Latino guy who longwindedly stated his support for the law as it now stands (i.e., undocumented kids who've at least gone to high school here are considered state residents), we probably would have pelted him with the grapes from the table.

Still, it was all a bit annoying. I swear the man positively lisped with sincerity as he cocked his head and made doe eyes to the room about how education is so important because he was a child with . . . dyslexia! It would probably eke out a victory over "broke a leg" and "dead grandmother" in *The Apprentice* home game of beating you over the head with the obstacles they've overcome, but so what? You're dyslexic, dude. Arnold Schwarzenegger had to overcome *being Arnold Schwarzenegger.*

On the way home, I called my favorite teacher, the one whose students' standardized test scores go up an average of 70 percent after she beats some sense into 'em: Commie Mom. "Hey, Jimmy and I are just coming from a Teachers for Westly event!" I told her.

"I hate that little fucking creep!" she murmured gently.

I explained: he wasn't creepy *per se*—well, he sort of was, but only because he was so fucking sincere—but he seemed nice enough, I guess, nicer than Schwarzenegger, anyway, though he did partner up with him on those stupid ballot measures (way to fire up your base, Steve!) and though he's still no Phil Angelides—especially since Angelides tops six feet. I called his press guy and asked.

The next night, my son and I were all set to go to a California Coalition for Immigration Reform meeting. "They're weirdoes who hate Mexican people," I explained. "It'll be fun!"

"But I don't hate Mexican people!" my son said, kinda all freaked out. "I like Mexican people! Do we have to go hang out with the weirdos?"

"No, son, we don't!" I decided. I don't help out in the office on Wednesdays.

SECTION FIVE

This Is the End

Last Call

Who killed Linda's Doll Hut? You did. And Kennedy

Linda Jemison would be the last person to point fingers, so I'll do it for her:

You killed Linda's Doll Hut. You, and you, and probably *you*. All those nights you showed up at her legendary Anaheim roadhouse and didn't buy beers. I was behind the bar at a Cadillac Tramps show. You people should have been *loaded*. But bartenders Yvette DeSpain and Greg Antista got to watch the entire show unmolested by pesky requests for drinks, with nothing to distract them from lead singer Gabby's enormous belly.

And then there were all those nights you didn't show up at all. Last year, almost no one attended the Alejandro Escovedo gig. Jesus, Thelonious Monster played to an empty house last month—Linda lost her ass on that one, promoting it six weeks in advance, for nada. You didn't show up for Hank Williams III either—probably, to be fair, because you figured he'd cancel again as he canceled his first two scheduled appearances. (He's got his granddaddy's legacy to live up to.)

And not just Linda's Doll Hut—your neglect has winged Club Mesa, too, with its punkrock quicksand floor that was almost as legendary as the vomit-stiffened carpets at the Hut. And Long Beach's Lava Lounge? Well, SnoopTown City Councilman Frank Colonna gets to mount its stuffed head on his wall, but I wouldn't be surprised if all of you were in cahoots. And whatever happened to In Cahoots, anyway? Is it still there? And where were you when they shot Kennedy? Kennedy killer!

And if you weren't enough: Disney construction diverted drivers around the

Doll Hut. Her core clientele aged, had babies, stayed home more often. Then there was the natural, undeniable pull of outside interests (bands to promote, a deal with Time Bomb records) and romance in Linda's life, forcing her to transform a one-woman operation into something a little more complicated. And expensive.

No, Linda (hereafter referred to as "Linda" in blithe disregard for Associated Press style because Linda does not need a last name in this county) will never point her finger at you or give you the bitch slap you deserve. She won't blame outside factors—not even Disneyland. It's not her style. And even if it were, she doesn't blame you anyway. This is not a story about what a well-respected and universally beloved sweetheart Linda is. For a thousand stories about that, do a Net search. This is a story about what she created. Linda's Doll Hut has been (as my colleague Jim Washburn said) the jewel in the belly button of OC's music scene for the past twelve years. And now it's time to bow out gracefully. Linda's Doll Hut will close its doors August 31.

A bunch of us are sitting in the small living room of Linda's pretty Fullerton apartment. While the Doll Hut may be a dank, windowless hole whose walls remain plumb only because generations of band stickers serve as mortar, Linda is, in fact, a girl. Her apartment is carpeted in springy greens instead of Coors. There are Winnie the Pooh toothbrush holders in the bathroom she shares with her grown niece, Ashley. There is a table full of lovely refreshments, and we are telling tales about the Hut.

Jimmy Camp, now the political director for the California Republican Party, was in the Earwigs, the first band to play the Doll Hut, a week after Linda opened it with her then-husband in 1989.

"This cute girl was fliering for her new bar," Camp says. "The fliers read, 'A beer bar by and for musicians.'" (Linda began drumming when she was twelve.)

Camp continues, "The grand opening had twenty-five-cent beers. Everyone we knew was there. We told her she needed music, but she said they weren't gonna have any. So we totally lied and told her we were from Austin and were only gonna be in town for a week. I told her I'd go to City Hall and take care of the permits and everything. I never did. We played all night."

That set the stage—or lack thereof in the case of Linda's Doll Hut where, through a kind of utilitarian aesthetic or democratic impulse, there is no stage, just a single, small floor bifurcated by the bar in a house that really is no bigger than a hut—for Social Distortion, Thelonious Monster, US Bombs, the Muffs, and Southern Culture on the Skids; for the Adolescents, Billy Zoom, Brian Setzer, Candye Kane and Everclear; for Exene and John Doe, Jonathan Richman, Hot Club of Cowtown, L7, Lee Rocker and Lit; for Mike Ness, Mike Martt and Mike Watt; for the Offspring, Reverend Horton Heat, Wayne Kramer, Weezer and the Supersuckers; for every band that's come out of Orange County. Linda gave people their first gigs straight from the garage. Big-time rock stars found at Linda's the chance to feel connected instead of bloated and isolated in their jewel-encrusted mansions.

"Tour managers and roadies for professional bands hate us!" Linda says with a laugh. "There's no stage, no back line, no dressing room, no food."

Steve Soto, who sometimes runs the door and used to handle Linda's band bookings, chimes in, "They wanna fax us a stage plot. We don't *have* a stage."

"A few bands pull up and go, 'Uh, we're gonna go get some food,'" she says. "They never come back."

When Bad Religion played—Soto guilted them into it after they recorded a song *very* similar to one by his band, the Adolescents—the band's management was expecting to roll in at 3 p.m. to take care of equipment and sound checks and all that. Um, there's really no need, guys. Just come back at 9 p.m., plug in and play.

In the old days, the place was a lunatic asylum. Regulars sat around in their underwear, watching porn and smoking cigars on Sundays, when the bar was closed.

Remember the time that girl punched Linda in the face? She had Linda down on the ground and was punching her and punching her until somebody Maced her.

Remember the time that guy pushed Linda? "Did he die?" someone asks.

Remember when CC was standing on the bar, hanging his ass out at everyone? Some guy stuck his finger right up there, like an experienced urologist performing CC's first prostate exam. CC's eyes lit up like a slot machine. He rounded on the poker, and the poker prepared for a fight but broke his ankle just standing up from his barstool. The two sat back down and kept drinking.

Remember the time the Cadillac Tramps' Gabby kicked that Marine's ass? The cops came, and Gabby sat down on the curb and started crying. "'I'm just a punker trying to go to the show, and he's fucking with me,'" Soto quotes Gabby as whining. Gabby peeked up, and one of the cops was Mexican-American. "'He called me a beaner,'" Soto recalls Gabby saying. The Marine went to jail.

But in twelve years, Linda says, that incident is one of just three times the cops had to be called. "We took care of it all in-house," she says.

Michael Eckerson, a graphic artist, insists no laws were ever broken. "There was never any nudity, ever. Jimmy never shot flares off the roof. And we *never* went over capacity." For anyone who's been wondering, the Hut's capacity is 49. Stop laughing!

In the fall of '98, the Alcoholic Beverage Control (ABC) reamed Linda's for a video game that had full-frontal nudity. The fine was $3,000, and they had to cancel a TSOL show because of it. The Hut was under surveillance for the next four months.

"They were the worst undercovers *ever*," Soto says. "They'd say things like, 'I bet you could get a lot of cocaine around here!' Or 'So, do you ever get these girls real drunk and take 'em out to the car . . . ?'" But Linda had her own Drug Enforcement Agency policy: meth guys—actually, any drug guys—were beaten and banished. Speed freaks are no fun.

The group remembers Pittner and Joe, the terrible alcoholics who worked at the machine shop across the street. Linda's Doll Hut had been open a while before she met the pair; they'd had a bet going to see who could stay on the wagon the longest. Finally, they both came over and declared the game ended.

Once, the two machinists were in the men's room for a long time before someone went looking for them. Pittner was peeing, and Joe was charging him with the vacuum cleaner. They were peeing on the walls and laughing and laughing.

The pair turned out to be object lessons for Doll Hut regulars. Eckerson says, "I used to work nearby, and I'd go to Linda's for a liquid lunch. It was a treat to go hang with those guys at the bar in the afternoons. But, man, you didn't want to grow up to be like them."

The group bickers over the wording of an actual quotation from Pittner. The closest they come is, "I'm not eating corn on the cob anymore 'cause when I shit myself in the shower, I gotta push the kernels down the drain with my toes."

Once, Linda was picking glass out of his head when he reached around and grabbed her ass. He always bragged about it afterward. When Pittner died after pretty much going on a mission to drink himself to death, his dog Bo curled up under a truck and died the same night.

The place isn't an asylum anymore—maybe because the punk rockers have become old punk rockers. And maybe that has something to do with declining bar revenue. Linda and her friends are thirty-six and wiser not twenty-four and stupid. They're marrying and having little punk rock babies. Mikey Hobbick recalls that he stalked Cher at the Hut for a year. "I said, 'Linda, you gotta get me a date with her!' She had a boyfriend, but he was in rehab."

Cher breaks in: "Mikey and Jimmy's number was actually on the wall in the ladies' room. 'For a good time call . . .'"

(Dave "The Chairman" Mau says his number, too, was on the women's room wall. The words above it read, "Dave will eat you all night long." For about three months, he kept getting giggling, drunken, 2:30 a.m. phone calls.)

Mikey and Cher's first date was at the Hut, on a Valentine's Day. There was champagne and flowers for the ladies. They have been married for almost three years and have a very nice little baby. And there are at least twenty couples like them, who met and married because of Linda's Doll Hut. "The marriages are lasting. That's the weird thing!" Linda exclaims. Rikk Agnew owns the Doll Hut couch on which his daughter was conceived, the crowd swears. There's a placard over it.

A few days later, Linda and her pretty niece Ashley are sitting by the pool behind her mom's house. Linda is talking about her debt, the red ink she acquired trying to keep the Doll Hut going. Once she was rear-ended, and the $20,000 settlement went straight into the Hut. When she used to scout bands for Time Bomb Records, her paychecks went straight to the Doll Hut's landlady.

"Maybe I'm not a very good businesswoman," she admits. And she's not speaking of the debt-ridden business she ran as a labor of love. Now that she's calling it quits, she doesn't want to sell the Hut but bury it. "Selling it would be the right thing to do from a business standpoint. I'm not about the money, but I need to get out of debt," she says. "My ego would love to think that no one else could do what I did." She laughs. "But not selling it would be like junking a car that still runs just so no one else could have it."

She seems to be thinking about it as we speak. She says she'll entertain offers and promises that if someone does what she did for the first six years—work behind the bar six nights a week and book the bands herself—money can and will be made. And if the place sells hard liquor—not just beer and wine—they'd make a mint. They'd have to take the name "Linda's" off the sign—it would be false advertising if they didn't—but the Doll Hut has a history dating back to 1957.

Linda's been thinking about it a lot: What went wrong? She's come to the conclusion that—once again—the Mouse is to blame. The Hut's financial difficulties started about three years ago, roughly the moment Caltrans began tearing up the offramps and onramps for the nearby 5 freeway. People couldn't figure out how to get there on any given day. I'd frequently leave Linda's at two in the morning, only to be shunted off the freeway within an exit or two—no signs, no arrows, just cars splintering off in twos and threes until all of a sudden, yours is the only car left, and you're staring at a scarred and scorched pit straight out of *Blade Runner*, with no earthly idea how to return to civilization. It was a nightmare, all so that Disneyland could get its own offramp and a facelift.

John Pantle, the Downtown Disney House of Blues' talent booker, agrees. "It's not the economy," he said. "Concerts do better in bad economies, as long as they're not the $40 or $50 tickets. You know what the best concert market in the country is? Detroit, and their economy's been in the shitter for fifteen years. And with Linda's, with a $5 cover, it's definitely not about that at all. It's all about location. Linda got screwed by her location."

Linda—who has paid for people's cab rides home for the past twelve years out of her own pocket; on whose couch so many broke or out-of-town rock stars crashed; who has thrown numberless benefits for worthy causes (most especially the Orangewood Children's Foundation) in the past decade—is telling me about a guy she once tossed out:

"He was the new singer for the Stains. They're all big Samoan guys, and he wasn't. I didn't realize who he was, and he ordered a beer, and I accidentally charged him for it instead of buying it for him. I didn't know, and he didn't say anything about it. So they go up to play, and I think, Oh, no, that guy's the new singer, and I didn't buy his beer! Before a word even comes out of his mouth, he kicks in my monitor and bashes my mic down on the bar, busting it."

He was immediately wrestled outside, but not before screaming at Linda, "YOU'RE A YUPPIE BITCH AND YOU MAKE LOVE TO YOUR MONEY!"

"I was furious," Linda says. "I was so mad I offered the bouncer fifty bucks to kick the guy's ass. But he wouldn't do it. He just said, 'Linda, you don't mean that.'"

A week later, the guy came back with a baseball cap down around his eyes.

"He was trying to be incognito," Linda says. "He said, 'I came in to apologize. . . . BUT YOU'RE A YUPPIE BITCH AND YOU MAKE LOVE TO YOUR MONEY!'"

These days, Linda is managing the band Wonderlove, a group of five nice boys with whom she's absolutely besotted—but not in a sexual way. She says she can and will make them famous. Their sound unplugged is beautiful, Beatles-esque melody. Plugged in, they're extremely loud—too loud for my ears.

"They have every element they need," Linda explains. "Bands I've worked with in the past have always been missing one of the elements, whether it's songwriting, or sobriety or just plain luck. They have it all. And they're not self-sabotaging!"

Linda's golden-brown eyes are sparkling. She actually glows when she talks about Wonderlove, as she does when she talks about a man she's seeing who, shockingly, is neither a musician nor from Texas. It's clear she's not a bit sad; it's everyone else who's whining and moaning. She's excited to be able to devote her time to mothering these boys and, she says, "nurturing my personal life."

But the rest of us will no longer have the dirty, vile roadhouse in which to run into our friends and see the latest bitchen San Francisco punk band or a sweaty set by some Austin roots rockers. We won't see Dexter Holland crowd-surf straight through the ceiling tiles (he sweetly sent her a check to cover the repairs). The rockabilly kids no longer have a place to go, dressed to kill, every Thursday night to see Big Sandy or Russell Scott when no other venues would bother with greaser music. There will be no place to go after the Hootenanny, when people like John Doe and the Reverend Horton Heat would come and make music and drink beer after the sun went down.

Things change and scenes die. New ones come along. Entropy and rebirth. Jimi Hendrix played the Golden Bear; it was shuttered in 1986. Johnny Cash played the Foothill; owner Ron Price sold it to a salsa outfit last year. And now, someone else will look at the sea of kids with nowhere to go and decide there's a need to be met. And maybe they'll even do so with Linda's hallmarks of kindness and respect.

Say goodnight, Gracie.

We All Lose Things

Two Thursdays ago, the night before she went in for her C-section, my sister Sarah called me to say goodbye.

"You know, in case I die tomorrow," she said.

"Don't die, Sarah!" I instructed her sternly.

"Thank you!" she exclaimed. "You're the first person who's said that!"

"That's because everyone else sucks," I gently explained.

With my little niecelets a whopping week old, I made it this weekend out to Surprise, Arizona, with my buttercup of a son and Commie Mom, to get a gander. Sadie was all Jewy and dark and squished and lopsided like Shannen Doherty from hanging out upside-down on Sarah's cervix for the past three months (each contraction massaging her head into a Nefertiti oblong), while Sabrina was a delicate WASPy rosebud who had spent her gestation reclining peacefully with her head on one kidney and her feet on the other.

By the time Sarah popped them out, she really could have kicked it. Her system was going toxic from her organs shutting down thanks to two—two!—babies stomping on them with all their 19 inches each, and she had a terrifying edema that had swollen her entire body until her feet looked like loaves of Roman Meal. Nor could you see that she'd once owned knees.

It was way more than a hundred degrees in Surprise, the pretty city to which I *told* my sister not to move when she'd be seven months pregnant with twins. In July. In Arizona. Where every restaurant's a chain—does a restaurant really *need* to be the size of a Home Depot?—and everything looks like Mission Viejo. Where the town that had ten thousand people ten years ago has one hundred thousand today. Where new tracts are being built scores at a time, houses built to within inches of one another. Where people are buying those homes with interest-only loans, and where those people are stupid and she didn't know anybody and she'd be housebound and crazy and pregnant with twins in July in Arizona.

She and her husband did it anyway (I blame her husband). But despite all that, I have to say: the town's xeriscaping is *amazing*, vivid desert flowers blooming like fire and mesquite trees lacy and green in the stifling air.

And thank the good lord, my sister didn't die.

Of course, she still might die of boredom.

I had envisioned my sister dying in childbirth even before she called to tell me goodbye. It would be just like her, and then I'd have to take in her twins, and how the hell would I raise two more babies all on my own?

I was feeling, as usual, quite sorry for me.

And here's a little secret: I like to imagine the deaths of people I love, and I do it all the time. Like Holly Hunter in *Broadcast News*, it helps me have a nice little cry. I envision the moment I hear the news; I imagine my screaming and shaking and martyrdom. I feel the seismic magnitude of my bereftness, everything around me as still as the Arizona air. This works best when envisioning the death of my child, though usually I feel guilty about that and substitute a maiming or horrible brain damage, when he's not escaping harm through my lionesslike mother's love and I get shot in the face in his stead.

It's all very cinematic. And it ain't even close.

Last week, Rush Limbaugh said of Cindy Sheehan, "I'm weary of even having to express sympathy. We all . . . We *all* lose things." It's true. I lost a stuffed animal on Amtrak in Kansas when I was six, and I totally still remember that. I also lost a bet against my son this weekend when I said Knoxville was the capital of Tennessee. I lose my keys pretty often (my boy always helps me find them), and at least twice I've lost my wallet (what a godforsaken ass-pain that is!), and I lost my virginity when I was sixteen. I've definitely lost a boyfriend or two who didn't know that *by law* no one's ever allowed to leave me (whether or not I'd told them to) and who need to man up and give me a call (whether or not that's a good idea). And of course Rush Limbaugh's lost his mind.

What a waste it is to lose one's mind, indeed.

I haven't lost a child, but the details are all worked out if I ever should. I did watch my mom lose my older brother, though, when he was twenty-one. She was a mess for years and years, and even now, fifteen years on, she probably just keeps it hidden. I know she thinks about him all the time. I remember being embarrassed for her when she was standing in my dad and stepmom's kitchen, talking at my stepmom's parents about her beautiful son. I saw their sympathy as they listened, but I figured they were mortified, and I wished she would just stop.

For anybody who says the Left is "grief-pimping," they should take their heads out of their asses: Cindy Sheehan is holding up *amazingly*, and it's because—unlike the president—she's actually *got* a noble cause.

I've seen some terrible quotes this week, and a lot of them are from persnickety Dems such as Mickey Kaus and the DLC, for whom nothing's ever good enough, distancing themselves from this one-woman force. They don't like the people flocking to her; they don't like the apocryphal statements she never made; hell, the DLC—the Democratic Leadership Council!—doesn't like that, like more than half of America now, the woman is *against the war*.

We all lose things. What are we going to find in their place?

Bring 'em On

The six of us on the puddle-jumper from Houston to Waco had to sit in the back to keep it from nose-diving. Nobody cared for the thought, or the turbulence. But it was a friendly group, united and bonded in fear, and the old man wearing the US Army Retired ball cap and flag lapel pin was happy to answer when the young, pretty black girl who said she majors in political science asked him what he thought about what was going on . . . she said it shyly . . . *"over there."*

"We never should have gone there in the first place," he said, dry and crotchety but matter-of-fact. "The whole thing was based on lies."

It wasn't the answer I expected from an old coot in Texas.

I was on my way to Crawford to see the president, and I did: I saw him Saturday night on the TV from my perch in the bar at the Waco Hilton. He was taking in the nearby Little League game with Condi—and Laura in the center seat *for the block.* I got a sight better look at him than America's newest Public Enemy No. 1, Cindy Sheehan, did, camped as she was in a ditch and utterly lacking either TV or bar. All she saw of him was his motorcade—and behind those tinted windows, he was probably giving her the finger.

The president looked happy, relaxed, pretty great, and he should have: his schedule that day had included a nap, lunch with Condi, some fishing, some "reading," a two-hour bike ride with reporters, and the Little League game.

It did not include a trip to Camp Casey.

The gravel lane off Prairie Chapel Road is still a couple of miles from the president's Crawford spread, but it's as close as the Secret Service will let Cindy

Sheehan get. And around Sheehan has sprung a movement; perhaps you've seen it on the TV your own bad self! Named for her son Casey, who died in Iraq a year ago after volunteering for a rescue mission, the encampment of folks includes a lot of signs and a lot of milling about. There are tents crammed between the lane and barbed wire and booths piled high with food. There is also a beautiful installation by Arlington West, featuring more than 800 small white crosses, inscribed with the names of fallen soldiers and lovingly tended with flowers and flags.

There ain't much to do at the side of a Texas prairie, except flirt with the photogs and the special agents, and I was pretty much the only person doing that, so there's a lot of time to be killed (and made): the tall, soft-spoken, unglamorous Sheehan, who this week has been called a kook, a nutball, a traitor and a whore and whose husband on Friday filed for divorce (really, she's just had one hell of a week), has vowed to stay at the side of the road outside Crawford all of the president's five-week vacation or until he scoots out to talk to her, whichever comes first. And I have a sneaking suspicion as to which one will.

But if the president wasn't heeding Sheehan's call, about three hundred other people were. Maybe it was four hundred—it was hard to tell: at any one time about half were at Camp Casey and half were back at the Crawford Peace House, shielding themselves from the 100-degree heat on the grass under grand old trees, walking the labyrinth of the stone mandala, or pitching in to unload gifts and supplies people had trucked in.

While one guy at the Peace House asked, "Who wants twenty cases of Coke?" to general lefty apathy, another laughed about the "lesbian agenda," and a woman with a five o'clock shadow coordinated *something* very efficiently. Loaded buffet tables stood in rows in a tent, and people from Minnesota and Louisiana and Pennsylvania and Florida and lots and lots of Texans wandered among them, making time and killing it at once.

They'd all come to rally with this woman, this regular lady, who's not particularly camera-ready but who's agreed to be The Face anyway—and by "agreed," I mean a *tacit* agreement, an *organic* one, like every piece of fruit served at this damn place. No professionals have come to Sheehan and drafted her to be a spokeswoman, she just became one, and people—including professional organizers like the peace chicks of Code Pink—have flocked around her to help.

Well, for the most part. An awful lot of people are also flocking onto the television to call this woman with a dead son names.

My boyfriend had broken up with me for breaking up with him, even though I totally took it back, so I figured the Hilton, with the press corps, was the perfect place to be. And it was, though I just ended up with a new posse of married guys. As we watched the Raiders on one screen and Bush on another, Charlie, an old sound guy from ABC, said he loves covering George because he never runs late. When I wrote down that he said that the trains ran on time, Charlie threatened to complain to my editor. It was something about journalistic ethics, which is of course hilarious, and it made me laugh and laugh. I yelled at the mainstream reporters about lots of other stuff—Siragusa came up, as Siragusa is wont to do, but that one call during that Patriots game (*you* know the one!) came up too.

But switching to Scotch with my new AP pal was only a good idea till Sunday morning, when I woke up with eyes like beeyootiful rubies in my dank little dump of a Motel Six.

Back at Camp Casey during Sunday morning's super-ecumenical prayer service (a rabbi, a priest and an imam walk into a bar . . .), Crazy Larry across the road decided to shoot off rounds from his shotgun. "I'm getting ready for dove season," he told the instalanche of cameramen, although since none of them used to date a fireman, none of them knew dove season starts September 1, and then he started ranting about the Port-A-Potties down the lane and out of sight, next to which thoughtful folks had piled new boxes of baby wipes and bottled water and antibacterial soap. "It's the battle of the Port-A-Potties!" he crowed, while our new buddy Ed from the Secret Service showed just how valuable diplomacy can be. "Sir, are you all right? Do you need to sit down? How about a cold cloth for your forehead?" he intoned, while another agent was on his headset with a supervisor. "No, we did *not* authorize any shots," he replied to what was surely a ration of shit.

After Crazy Larry left, a TV-ready Amurrican family joined the lonely counterprotester across the road, the one with the sign reading "Sheehanistan: American Haters [*sic*] Welcome." The *GQ*-cowboy dad told reporters he had to fly for work after 9/11, and he hadn't let the terrorists stop 'im. "What do you do for work?" someone asked—probably my buddy at the *Oakland Tribune*, since he was the only reporter actually working. The rest, who for all of the weekend would remain unseen, manned the air conditioner back at the press center or maybe took a pleasure drive through Crawford's just-flat-gorgeous fields. "I'm an automobile auctioneer," proudly answered *GQ*, part of the thin blue line of auto auctioneers between us and the terrorists, keeping it real and keeping us safe. His little boy, in cammies, waved a plastic AK.

A lot is being made on the blogs and on the talk shows about the co-opting of Cindy Sheehan by "the Left." *These are the fringe groups,* they're snarling, *the far Left!*—and yeah, People for the Ethical Treatment of Animals were there. But a lot of the guys at Camp Casey were Vietnam vets, while the rest were pretty middle-aged and wholesome, middle-class and earnest. People ate meat, and smoked cigarettes, and drove cars with internal combustion engines. Aside from the fact that there were recycling bins, even in the middle of a field, it really was awfully mainstream—and with more than half of Americans now saying Iraq wasn't worth it, now "the mainstream" is us. Of course, at Sunday's lunch at the Peace House—a gorgeous Middle Eastern buffet, hosted by a group of Iraqi-Americans who fed the multitudes like Jesus with loaves and fishes— I did have a particularly crunchy exchange.

"So the Iraqi women made this beautiful lunch for us!" the woman sitting next to me lilted over her lavash. "Have you met any of them yet?"

"They're in the kitchen," I answered, *clearly joking,* and because the sentence demanded it, added, "where they belong!"

"Oh, *nooo!*" she reproved me, shocked and distraught.

Okay, whatever, San Francisco.

Luckily, there were some smart-ass dudes from Austin, listening to Willie

Nelson and drinking Lone Stars by their truck, with whom to steal beers and make fun of her, while back in town, some bikers across the tracks from the Peace House were made to take down their signs calling the protesters *pussies*. Sorry, dudes. I guess freedom of speech isn't free.

I'd been worried about Sheehan sleeping by the side of the road. With all these yahoos yahooin' all over the place, I figured it wouldn't be long before someone took a shot at her instead of into the hot, still air, and the Crawford sheriff agreed. He asked her to stay down at the Peace House by nights.

And the night I left, a 46-year-old real-estate agent in a pickup truck drove a beeline to her tent. She wasn't there, but the "Arlington of Crawford" was, and he smashed more than 500 of the 800 little white crosses, with flowers and flags, that bore witness to our dead.

I wonder about the pundits who call Cindy Sheehan a traitor. I wonder what they think of that.

Cockfight!

Charley's Last Stand: Music, Booze, Food and Fun was right across the street from our Oklahoma City Howard Johnson. There wasn't any way my little brother and I weren't going.

"Don't go to Booze and Fun!" Commie Mom implored from in front of the Alito hearings rerunning on C-SPAN. We'd already checked Fox News to see, as my little brother said, if they were being right-wing right this very minute! Surprise! They were!

"We have to go to Booze and Fun!" we explained. "You can't not go to Booze and Fun! It's the law!"

And we did. It was pretty much the same as going to an AA meeting anyway.

I saddled up and ordered my cranberry and soda; Cakeyboy kept to just two vodka tonics. The lady bartender carded his 23-year-old long-haired gorgeous Malibu self—like he was the star of a Hollywood movie—but not me. "It's because you're so old," he chirruped delightedly. "You're Oldie Hawn!"

"That's no way to get laid," our lady bartender drawled, to our simultaneous horrified screams of "I'm his sister!" and "She's my sister!" This made Skanky Brenda, sitting at the bar, very, very glad, despite the fact that her son, she said, is twenty-seven.

"Y'all wanna go to a titty bar?" Skanky Brenda asked me after Cake and I had been playing pool a while. "There's one right in walking distance!" I was kind. "We have an early flight back home," I murmured. "But thank you." Later, walking back across the street, I told John about Skanky Brenda's invite. "She wanted to get you all horny at the titty bar and then have her way with you!" I shrieked. "I saved you from Skanky Brenda!"

"Aw, thanks, Becca!" my little brother said, and I could tell he was touched, though not like Skanky Brenda would have touched him. I couldn't wait to get back to the hotel and tell my mom about our Chuckie Booze's adventure! But it was 10 p.m., so she was sound asleep.

We had a good time, my mom, my little brother and I, jet-setting to the Bible Belt for a thirty-six-hour stay. We giggled so hard on the midnight plane from Vegas at the flight attendant who sounded like he was speaking Tagalog, hurrying like an auctioneer through the longest safety announcement in history—he was trading back and forth with a flight attendant who sounded like she was from Belize for going on fifteen minutes, and every two minutes or so we'd recognize a single word ("seatbelt!")—that my mom went from trying to frown us into silence to having an asthma attack from laughing too hard herself. The flight attendant, who was standing behind us at the back of the plane, started to laugh too.

Our cabbie, at 3 a.m. Oklahoma time, was a giant cauliflower ear dressed as a man. He mush-mouthed his way through an explanation of why people from California weren't welcome in Oklahoma. "Boomhauerboomhauerboomhauer Environmental Protection Agency!" he said. "Boomhauerboomhauerboomhauer-COCKFIGHTS!" said he. From what we could gather, he was upset that people from California were coming in with their money, paying for advertising trying to ban cockfights in OKC.

"I'm sorry," my mother said, not sorry at all. "But we are going to have a fight!" Sometimes when my mother is fighting with strangers, I soothe her down. Not this time. "I think you should!" I said. This guy was a prick!

We told him my mom had grown up in Oklahoma, and she was a Democrat even then. We didn't tell him we were there because her little brother had died.

My mom made me tip him $7 on our $13 cab ride, to prove, she said, a point. I think, pissed as he was about California big shots throwing around their money, that we probably proved his instead. That meant that on our return ride, when our cabby was actually a gentleman, kind, and looked just like *The Big Lebowski*'s The Dude, I had to tip him just the same. What kind of point would we have proved rewarding a man more for being an asshole than for being friendly and kind?

We went and saw our Uncle Davey off. He had been brilliant and loving, but always terribly sad. It was our second Oklahoma funeral in as many years. We'd been there a couple of Fourths ago to sing to our grandma at her death in her little twin bed. That trip had been a nightmare: the women quietly did what needed to be done, while the men didn't know how to do anything but beat fuck-all out of each other. My little brother, after a beating from my older one, had threatened to steal my mom's rental car and drive it back to Cali. Meanwhile, frail, tiny Grandma Jeanie had been too strong to die. When it was my turn to sit up with her, while my mom and aunt pretended for an hour to at least *try* to sleep, she would stop breathing for going on a minute, until I thought she had finally passed, and then she would gasp again. I nearly had a heart attack each time. "Mom!" I said, sure my grandmother had been waiting for just this, and it had only just occurred to us, "Let's say the Rosary!" We did, my Aunt Annie (formerly my Uncle Johnny) coming in quietly to join us. Uncle Davey had just walked into the apartment too, and he came in and started intoning the Hail Marys and Our Fathers alongside us. I was sure that the moment we finished, her spirit would be free.

Instead, it was another day wetting her lips with a Q-tip while she struggled to breathe.

We weren't there when Uncle Davey died of his cancer. He didn't want a bunch of people sitting around with nothing to do. It probably saved a lot of ass-beatings for the men.

We had a good time. My little brother was sweet and funny and kept our spirits up. We responded by ragging on him about his pants, which were constantly falling all the way under his bare butt, and my mom picked at him about his hair too (it's just how we show we care), but I thought it looked good. My mom's retiring in a couple of years from her teaching job in South Central, where she's been indoctrinating third-graders into communism while also raising their test scores an average of 70 percent for sixteen years running. She has property outside Tecumseh, bought with a settlement from the city of Manhattan

Beach after one of their cops roughed up her then-57-year-old schoolteacher self. Uncle Davey was going to help her drill her well.

Most of the family's moved to Dallas now. My mom wants me to move to OKC, where I'd be just an hour's drive. They even have an alt.-weekly, of a sort. It wasn't very good. "You can fix it!" my mom suggested sunnily. No. No, I can't. I've been bitching about Orange County because it's too backward and conservative, and *Oklahoma City*'s gonna be the place I thrive? Boomhauer-boomhauerboomhauerEPA?

Mama, I love you, but fuck that.

Bullet Dodged!

I had just walked my son to his first day of junior high and helped him get his schedule when I realized there were only about two other moms in sight. "Okay, go find your classes," I told him. Sink or swim, fucker!

Then, on the way home, and with a flashback to the first day of kindergarten, I cried, just a tiny.

A few hours later, a co-ex of mine called up and asked me if I was marrying our mutual ex-boyfriend. She'd heard a wedding was in the works and thought it might be to me, but thank the good and loving lord, it wasn't. Bullet dodged!

That afternoon, my mom called and said my cousin had died. He was a frightening kid, really messed up, and it wasn't a surprise, but I cried.

The next day my little brother Cakeyboy had a grand mal seizure at the side of the road after he got off the bus from school. He was unconscious for thirty minutes, and when he woke, he thought the paramedics at his side were CIA guys come to take him to Guantanamo.

And I worried about him and I cried and cried.

It was the perfect time to jet off to *Riviera*'s anniversary party.

Now, I hate *Riviera* magazine, honestly. It's run by one of my very best friends, Kedric Francis, who this year finally saw fit to add me to the sexy list (he'd had eight years to add me to the 20 in Their 20s when he was at *OC Metro* from the time we met until I got too old, and several more years after that to include me in some List of Hotness or other), and I hope you saw the picture. I'm convinced I looked like Brigitte Bardot, all naked and in bed. But the magazine, while beautiful to look at (especially with me in it), is like Exhibit A in How To Start Class Warfare With Your Friends and Neighbors. It's for Newport people, and it reads as such. Its very first issue, just five years ago now, included stories on Tiffany, and throwing thousand-dollar tea parties for your four-year-old princess, and columns on "Why We Live on the Riv." That launch party, five years ago, came two days after September 11.

There were canapés that September 13, and I enjoyed them, and it was probably good to get out of my house and actually interact with people, but I needed at the time to be back in bed with my television on, the TV news pumped directly into my veins, playing a little game I like to call "Did They Confirm That?" (correct answer: No) and weeping and sobbing and sitting shiva for the prescribed seven days.

I was grieving, but I was also frightened—terrorized, really; it worked, I guess—and wished my boyfriend—the one who's getting married, not to me, bullet dodged, thanks et cetera—would bring his gun to my house so when society unraveled and mobs of looters came, he could shoot them for me, or at least brandish the thing. He went backpacking for a week in the mountains instead.

Now do you see what I mean?

Then, one day, I got over it. I'm the person the Right talks about when they say Americans haven't learned the lesson of 9/11: I'm not scared of terrorists, even though I'm pretty sure they'll hit us again, and again. I'm not "vigilant," and I don't care to be. I don't spend my days seething about Islamo-Fascists trying to wipe America off the map. I don't think multiculturalism weakened America, and I think people who say so are retarded. (And what multiculturalism has to do with 9/11 confounds my puny liberal brain, but I don't get the connection between 9/11 and homosexuality and feminism either, as Falwell does, or the connection between 9/11 and promiscuity, with noted thinker Dinesh D'Souza saying Al Qaeda was right to be disgusted by our freedoms. If you ask me, and you implied that you did when you picked up this book, Falwell and D'Souza would be happier in Afghanistan.)

I may not be booking a vacation to Beirut (or even Spain), but I'm pretty sure I'm okay here, even if my mom does live right on top of the Port of LA and I can practically spit on the Matterhorn. I don't think we're facing the most terrifying enemy we've ever known: one in a long list of people the US said were "madmen" with whom we could never negotiate because they were just too fucking crazy: Khrushchev, Qaddafi, Saddam, Noriega, now that unpronounceable guy from Iran. You know: the one who now wants to negotiate with us over their nuclear program.

We always have an enemy. We like to. Fear and violence stimulate the reptilian, primitive part of the brain. But the rest of the entire world thinks President Bush is the madman now, and you'd think we'd take pause to consider that instead of just planning for our next title-weight bout.

Looking at you, Iran! And Syria, don't get too cozy!

Because if there's anyone you'd trust to prosecute a war, it's our War President, President Bush.

So I went to the *Riviera* anniversary party. I thought about my cousin and my brother and my stupid ex-boyfriend (him I wasn't sad about), and I didn't think about September 11 at all, or the terrorists would have won.

The DJ was excellent, starting with some Brazilian pop and mambo, segueing into some lazy French hip-shakers, and then moving into funk and old school. The food was excellent, and copious. And despite four hundred of *Riviera*'s closest and richest friends standing in attendance, there was never a wait for champagne.

And I danced and danced for two hours, until my son reminded me it was a school night, and would I like to go home?

On September 11, just a few days later, I took him to a ball game. The Angels lost to the White Sox, but it was close and featured some great double plays. I missed the tribute beforehand to the attack on our homeland, because I didn't really care.